HEARTFELT

PIPPA MIDDLETON

IN PARTNERSHIP WITH

British Heart
Foundation

The British Heart Foundation (BHF) funds life-saving research to improve the diagnosis, treatment and prevention of cardiovascular disease.

Pippa Middleton has been an Ambassador for the charity since 2014. Bringing her passion for sport, adventure – and now food – to the role, Pippa has helped raise vital funds and awareness of heart health.

Featuring over 100 delicious, heart-healthy recipes, this book is a collaboration between Pippa and the BHF, all proceeds going to the charity to help fund future research.

"We can't thank Pippa enough for her generous donation of time and effort. Her support, dedication and passion for everything she does for the BHF really is life-changing."

Simon Gillespie
Chief Executive, British Heart Foundation

A HEARTFELT HELLO

Helping to produce this book has been the greatest pleasure for me, bringing together two of the things I care about most – delicious food and healthy living. In fact, I am passionate about both. And I care deeply about the charity which is publishing this book and of which I am an Ambassador – the British Heart Foundation. The work of the BHF is really important. Coronary heart disease is still Britain's biggest single cause of death, with more than twice as many women dying from this condition as from breast cancer.

Healthy eating is something which all of us strive for, even if we sometimes stray. Whether it's an occasional guilty pleasure or a daily habit, we feel uncomfortable when we eat something we know we shouldn't. This collection of recipes is not intended to heighten that discomfort. Far from it. Those of us who put this collection together wanted to demonstrate how easy it is to create simple dishes using everyday ingredients which, in addition to being delicious, are also the sort of food recommended by dietitians for those with a heart condition, or for those at risk of one.

I have worked alongside a team of experts in the production of this book, starting with the Waitrose Weekend Food Editors, who helped to create the recipes and have been supportive throughout. BHF's registered dietitians have also advised me throughout the process, and each of the recipes has been analysed for its nutritional content. Finally, they have been road-tested for cooking practicality and deliciousness. Each works not just in taste but also in the provision of energy and sustenance for an active life. We are all delighted to recommend them.

In the making of Heartfelt it was an honour to meet a group of amazing individuals who have been affected by heart conditions. Over a very special lunch they shared their moving stories with me, stories I am proud to share with you throughout this book.

I like to think that activity defines my life. Ever since school, sport has been essential to me, and I am inspired by sportsmen and women who are at the top of their game. Some exceptional sporting greats, including Roger Federer, Lewis Hamilton and Alistair Brownlee, have, as you will see, been kind enough to offer their support to this collection of recipes, for which I am very grateful.

I not only love to watch sport, I like to be active, too. In recent years, I have regularly participated in testing physical events which I describe as my 'adventures'. I do these for fun, and often also to raise money for the charities I support.

Completing those adventures requires a great deal of hard work and preparation, and diet is an essential element in that process. Each challenge is different, but all have a common theme of health awareness and preparedness. The right food is an essential component of good preparation.

I hope that readers will benefit not only from a growing awareness of health from this book but also from the idea that healthy food is not just good for you, but can also be fun to prepare and delicious to eat. Thank you for buying this copy. And thank you, too, for supporting the work of the BHF.

Pippa Middleton

9 ♥

THE FOUNDATION OF A HEALTHY HEART

Healthy eating is for everyone. You don't need a family history of cardiovascular disease to start looking after your body today, and eating right is one of the simplest, most empowering ways to do that. For most of us eating is not just about health – it's about *pleasure*. These recipes have been created so that you can be inspired and create delicious food that will also help keep your heart healthy.

WHAT IS CARDIOVASCULAR DISEASE?

Cardiovascular disease (CVD) is an umbrella term that describes all diseases of the heart and circulation. It includes everything from conditions that are diagnosed at birth, or inherited, to health problems such as stroke and coronary heart disease.

Modifiable risk factors (like smoking, physical inactivity and poor diet) can contribute significantly to our risk of CVD. So whether you've already been diagnosed with a condition or want to protect your health for the future, making the right lifestyle choices now can help.

WHERE DO I BEGIN?

It's easy to feel daunted if you think your lifestyle needs big changes. No worries: start small! Choose the one thing you most want to change and begin there. As you get used to each adjustment, make the next one – stick with it and you'll be surprised by how quickly they add up to big results.

Below are a few suggestions for how you can change your diet to help look after your heart. Remember that other factors in your lifestyle are also important. Being physically active, stopping smoking and maintaining a healthy weight will also reduce your risk, as will making sure you take any medications you're prescribed.

HOW TO EAT WELL

The types of food you choose – in the right amounts – can help you maintain a healthy weight, and reduce your risk of developing type 2 diabetes, high blood pressure and high cholesterol. They can also help you manage these conditions if you already have them.

If you're worried that eating healthily will mean a life of restriction and excluding all your favourite foods, don't be. It's about eating the foods that give your body the nutrients it needs to stay healthy while also being enjoyable. By making small, sustainable changes – tweaks to make the food you normally enjoy healthier rather than a radical overhaul – you can fit heart-healthy food into your life without missing out on the social aspects of eating that make it such a pleasure.

There's no need to exclude any specific foods; it's the overall balance of your diet that is important, not particular meals or nutrients. Grouping foods in the way we describe here is helpful because each category contributes different nutrients to our diet. But the trick is to make sure we get more of some food groups and less of others – not to cut out any one group completely.

The traditional Mediterranean diet can be a helpful way to visualise what a healthy diet looks like. It's associated with lower rates of coronary heart disease and type 2 diabetes, as well as helping maintain a healthy weight. A Mediterranean diet includes plenty of fruit and vegetables, wholegrain starchy foods, pulses, white and oily fish, unsaturated oils (most famously olive oil), nuts and seeds.

The key is not to obsess over what you ought to cut down on but instead focus on making sure you eat enough of the foods you need to eat more of. By doing this you'll find that there is less room in your diet for foods like butter, cheese, fatty meats, cakes and pastries, which are high in saturated fat, salt and sugar.

FRUITS AND VEGETABLES

Eating at least five 80g portions of fruit and veg a day is linked to a lower risk of coronary heart disease and stroke. Fruit and vegetables should make up over a third of the food we eat each day. They provide us with fibre, which helps keep our digestive systems healthy, as well as vitamins and minerals.

WHAT COUNTS?

To count towards your five a day, fruits and vegetables can be fresh, frozen, tinned (in juice or water), dried or juiced (once a day). An adult portion is 80g of fresh, frozen or tinned fruits or vegetables (use a handful as a rough guide), 30g of dried fruits or 150ml of juice. Pulses such as kidney beans, chickpeas and haricot beans can also be included in your five a day – they only count as one portion, though, no matter how much you eat.

Juices and smoothies contain vitamins and minerals, which make them a better choice than sugar-sweetened drinks, but the juicing process releases lots of natural sugars. The number of calories they add to your diet can mount up quickly, so it's a good idea to watch how much you drink. Juices and smoothies do count towards your five a day, but only once a day, and a portion size is 150ml or a quarter of a pint.

EASY WAYS TO INCLUDE MORE FRUIT & VEG

* Sweeten porridge or cereal with chopped, fresh or dried fruit instead of sugar, syrups or honey.

* For a more nutritious option than biscuits or crisps, snack on apple slices with a tablespoon of Nut Butter | page 33 |, or carrot sticks with a delicious Roasted Cucumber Tzatziki | page 67 | or Homemade Houmous | page 73 |.

* Get into the habit of having fruit and veg as a main part of your meals. Try a salad or a chunky vegetable soup for lunch and make sure you have a couple of portions of veg or salad alongside main meals.

* Throw a handful of extra chopped vegetables or pulses into soups and stews. They'll add texture and flavour as well as nutrients.

* End your meals with fruit. Try stewing and baking all kinds of fruit as well as eating it fresh, and top with a dollop of low-fat natural yoghurt.

STARCHY CARBOHYDRATES

Starchy carbohydrate foods such as rice, pasta, potatoes and bread give us energy, vitamins and minerals. They're also an important source of fibre, which helps keep our digestive system healthy and can contribute to reducing cholesterol levels.

WHAT COUNTS?

Starchy foods include grains such as oats, rice, wheat, bulgur wheat and spelt, as well as the foods made from them, like pasta, breads and couscous. Sweet and white potatoes, yam and plantain are also included in this group. Leaving the skin on potatoes and choosing wholegrain versions of these foods will give you more benefits as well as flavour – they are higher in fibre and often contain more nutrients than white or refined starchy foods.

Like all carbohydrates, starchy foods provide energy. However, it's released more slowly than from sugars. Starchy foods also contain calcium, iron and B vitamins, and those high in soluble fibre, such as oats, can help lower cholesterol levels.

Starchy foods are often thought of as fattening, but that's partly down to how you cook them. To give you an example, 100g of boiled potatoes contains 74 calories, whereas the same sized portion of chips fried in oil contains 202 calories. You can keep the calories down without losing any of the comfort value by baking, boiling or steaming instead of frying, and by cutting down on how much fat you add.

PROTEIN

Two food groups provide us with our main sources of protein. These are dairy and dairy alternatives, and beans, pulses, fish, eggs, and meat. Protein helps the body's growth and repair, and maintains good overall health. A balance of protein from both these groups is important to ensure that we get enough iron and calcium in our diets.

DAIRY AND DAIRY ALTERNATIVES

Dairy products give us minerals like calcium, and vitamins including A and B12. However, the fat content varies greatly between foods in this group, and much of it is saturated. Choosing low-fat dairy options, such as semi-skimmed, 1% or skimmed milk, and low-fat products like quark and skyr (an Icelandic yoghurt similar to Greek yoghurt), will give you the nutrients with fewer calories and less saturated fat. In the long run this will help you stay at a healthy weight and maintain healthy cholesterol levels.

If you're dairy-free or just want to try something different, milk substitutes such as unsweetened soya, oat, rice and nut milks make a tasty alternative. If you're using them as a replacement for dairy, make sure they're fortified with calcium.

MEAT, FISH, EGGS AND NON-DAIRY PROTEIN

These foods are important because they contain protein, vitamins and minerals including iron. Even if you enjoy eating meat, leaving it out of a few meals each week is a good way to add more variety to your diet. Pulses are a healthy choice because they provide protein, fibre, vitamins and minerals but are low in fat. If you're veggie, it's important to include foods from this food group in your diet to help you avoid relying too heavily on dairy foods for protein. If you're not, and a completely meat-free meal seems like a step too far, try substituting just some of the meat in your dishes with pulses. This works well for casseroles, stews, curries and mince dishes – try our recipe for Beef & Lentil Cottage Pie | page 97 |.

It's also important to make room for fish in your diet. Aim for two portions a week, one of which should be oily fish because it contains a type of polyunsaturated omega-3 fatty acids that may help to prevent heart disease. Most of us could do with upping our weekly intake of fish, but pregnant and breastfeeding women and those planning a pregnancy should limit oily fish to no more than two portions a week and should completely avoid marlin, shark and swordfish as they may contain heavy metals and contaminants. Choosing sustainably sourced fish is also important – the **Marine Stewardship Council** website has more information on this (visit www.msc.org).

When it comes to eggs, there's no recommended limit for most people. They used to be restricted because they're a source of cholesterol but we now know that eating too much cholesterol is generally not the reason we develop high cholesterol in our bodies. For most people, the amount of saturated fat they eat is more of a problem. Feel free to enjoy eggs as part of a balanced diet, but try poaching or boiling them rather than frying, and avoid adding butter to scrambled eggs and omelettes.

People often avoid red meat to protect their hearts, but, with a couple of tweaks, there's really no need to completely cut it out. You can carry on enjoying red meat unless you eat more than 90g a day of red and processed meat, in which case it's recommended you cut down to 70g a day or less. For many of us it's simply about making healthier choices by choosing lean cuts of meat and removing the skin to limit saturated fat. When you buy processed meats like ham, bacon or sausages, check the nutritional information carefully to find the one with the least salt and saturated fat. Try just to eat them occasionally and in small amounts.

FAT, SUGAR AND SALT

Fatty, salty and sugary foods are often our favourites, but we don't actually need to eat them. Too much sugar and fat can mean we gain weight and too much salt is linked to high blood pressure. Some fat in the diet is essential to provide us with energy and fat-soluble vitamins. The problem is that we tend to eat too much saturated fat, which can lead to raised cholesterol levels – a risk factor for coronary heart disease.

TYPES OF FAT

All fats contain the same number of calories per gram. Fat is the most energy-dense nutrient so it's important to keep an eye on how much you eat. It's not just the amount of fat you need to pay attention to, though, but the type.

Eating too much saturated fat, which is in foods like butter, cream, cheese, pastry, biscuits, chocolate and fatty meats, is linked to raised cholesterol levels, which are a risk factor for coronary heart disease. In the UK, we eat more saturated fat than is recommended but we need to choose carefully what we replace it with when we cut down. Research suggests that replacing saturated fat with sugar or trans fats isn't beneficial to our heart health. Instead, the best replacement for saturated fat is unsaturated fat. This type of fat can be separated into two groups – monounsaturated and polyunsaturated.

Polyunsaturated fats include vegetable oils such as sunflower and corn oil, the spreads made from them, and the oils found in nuts and seeds including sunflower seeds, pine nuts and walnuts. The omega-3 oils in fish like mackerel, sardines, salmon and fresh (not tinned) tuna are also polyunsaturated. Monounsaturated fats are well known for their link to the Mediterranean diet. Olive oil, rapeseed oil, avocados, almonds, cashews, hazelnuts, peanuts and pistachios are all sources of monounsaturated fat.

HOW TO SWITCH TO HEALTHIER FATS
• Swap biscuits and chocolates for unsalted nuts.

• Use unsaturated oils like vegetable, rapeseed or olive oil for cooking.

• Have mashed avocado, rather than cheese, on wholegrain toast.

• Enjoy a portion of oily fish each week.

SUGARS
Like starchy foods, sugars give us energy. Unlike wholegrain starchy carbohydrates, though, foods high in added sugars often don't offer much else.

Diets that are high in sugar also tend to be high in energy, which can lead to weight gain if we don't use it up through activity. In the UK we eat too much sugar so most of us need to watch out for this. Generally adults should eat no more than 30g of sugar a day – that's the equivalent of 6 sugar cubes.

Sugars come in many forms – it's not just white sugar we need to look out for. Brown sugar, honey, syrups and nectars are all sugars. Look at ingredient labels; anything ending in *'-ose'*, for example fructose, is just another sugar that's been added. Sugars in juices and smoothies also count towards the limit.

Sweeteners such as honey, nectars and syrups may sound more natural but they are still added sugars. It's important to use these sparingly, too.

HOW TO CUT DOWN ON SUGARS
• Steer clear of sugary drinks. Instead, make water more tempting by piling it with ice and sliced oranges, lemon or cucumber and mint.

• Choose natural, low-fat yoghurt with chopped fresh or frozen fruit rather than sweetened, fruit-flavoured versions.

• Swap biscuits and cakes for unsweetened oatcakes, rice cakes or unsalted nuts.

• Use food labels to help you choose the products lowest in sugar.

SALT
Regularly eating too much salt is linked to raised blood pressure. The recommended maximum per day for an adult is 6g – about a teaspoon – and while intakes have reduced in recent years, we're still eating more than this in the UK. About 75% of the salt we eat is already in the food we buy, so it's important to check food labels to make the healthiest choices. Stick to products that are low in salt (0.3g per 100g or less) or sodium (0.1g per 100g or less) whenever possible.

Cooking from scratch is a great way to stay in control of how much salt we eat. Using less salt doesn't mean less flavour and, in fact, seasoning doesn't even have to mean salt. Instead, add lots of fresh or dried herbs, fresh chopped or dried chilli, dried spices such as cumin, coriander, smoked paprika, cinnamon and nutmeg, crushed or sliced garlic, lemon or orange zest and juice, finely chopped or sliced onions and black pepper.

It's not just table salt you need to watch out for, though. Fish sauce, soy sauce, chorizo, capers and olives are salty, too. That's not to say that these ingredients have to be avoided entirely, just keep an eye on the amount you use. As you get used to eating less salt you will probably find that your taste buds adjust.

Ready-made spice mixes, curry pastes and seasonings often also include salt, so make sure you check the label and use them sparingly, or use your own mixes made from individual dried spices so you know what's in them.

ARE YOU READY?

Hopefully the information in this section has provided a bit of an introduction to each of the food groups and how best to balance them for your health. Rethinking your diet and lifestyle can feel overwhelming at first but no one's expecting you to get it exactly right all the time. Remember to make small changes, one at a time, and focus on increasing the good things you eat rather than obsessing over what needs to be cut back on. I hope the recipes that follow help you to eat well and look after your heart health and that you enjoy sharing them with your loved ones.

Victoria Taylor.

Victoria Taylor
Senior Dietitian, British Heart Foundation

HOMEMADE STOCKS

Some of the recipes in this book call for the use of stock. Ideally, your stock should be homemade, as this will help to reduce the salt/sodium content of the dishes you prepare. Try the recipes for vegetable stock and chicken stock below. However, you can also use low-sodium stock cubes and powders, which are available in supermarkets.

VEGETABLE STOCK

MAKES APPROX. 600ML
PREPARE 15 MINS **COOK** 60 MINS

2 carrots, peeled and thinly sliced
2 onions, roughly chopped
2 sticks celery, roughly chopped
½ bulb fennel, roughly chopped
2 ripe tomatoes, diced
8 chestnut mushrooms, wiped clean and sliced
6 black peppercorns
1 bay leaf
Few sprigs fresh flat-leaf parsley

Put all the ingredients into a large saucepan and cover with about 850ml (1½ pints) water. Bring slowly to the boil, then cover and simmer very gently for 20–30 minutes. Strain and return to the saucepan.

Bring back to the boil and leave to bubble vigorously, uncovered, until the liquid has reduced by about a third. Allow to cool. Use this stock within 3 days or freeze.

To freeze: Pour the cooled stock into ice-cube trays and place in the freezer. When frozen, transfer the cubes to a bag, label and return to the freezer.

CHICKEN STOCK

MAKES APPROX. 600ML
PREPARE 10 MINS **COOK** 2 HOURS

Large pinch dried thyme
Small pinch dried sage
1 onion, roughly chopped
2 sticks celery, roughly chopped
1 chicken carcass

Put the herbs, onion and celery in a large saucepan. Chop or break the chicken carcass into rough pieces and drop into the pan. Pour in enough cold water to cover and bring to the boil. Reduce the heat to a gentle simmer, cover and leave to cook slowly for about 2 hours.

Check the level of liquid occasionally to ensure it doesn't dry out. Strain the stock into a heatproof container and leave to cool. Cover and chill the stock overnight in the refrigerator. It will set to a soft jelly.

Carefully skim off all the fat and scum that will have risen to the surface. Use this stock within 3 days or freeze as described under vegetable stock, left.

Note: Replace the chicken carcass with 1kg roasted beef bones for a beef stock.

I HEA
BREA

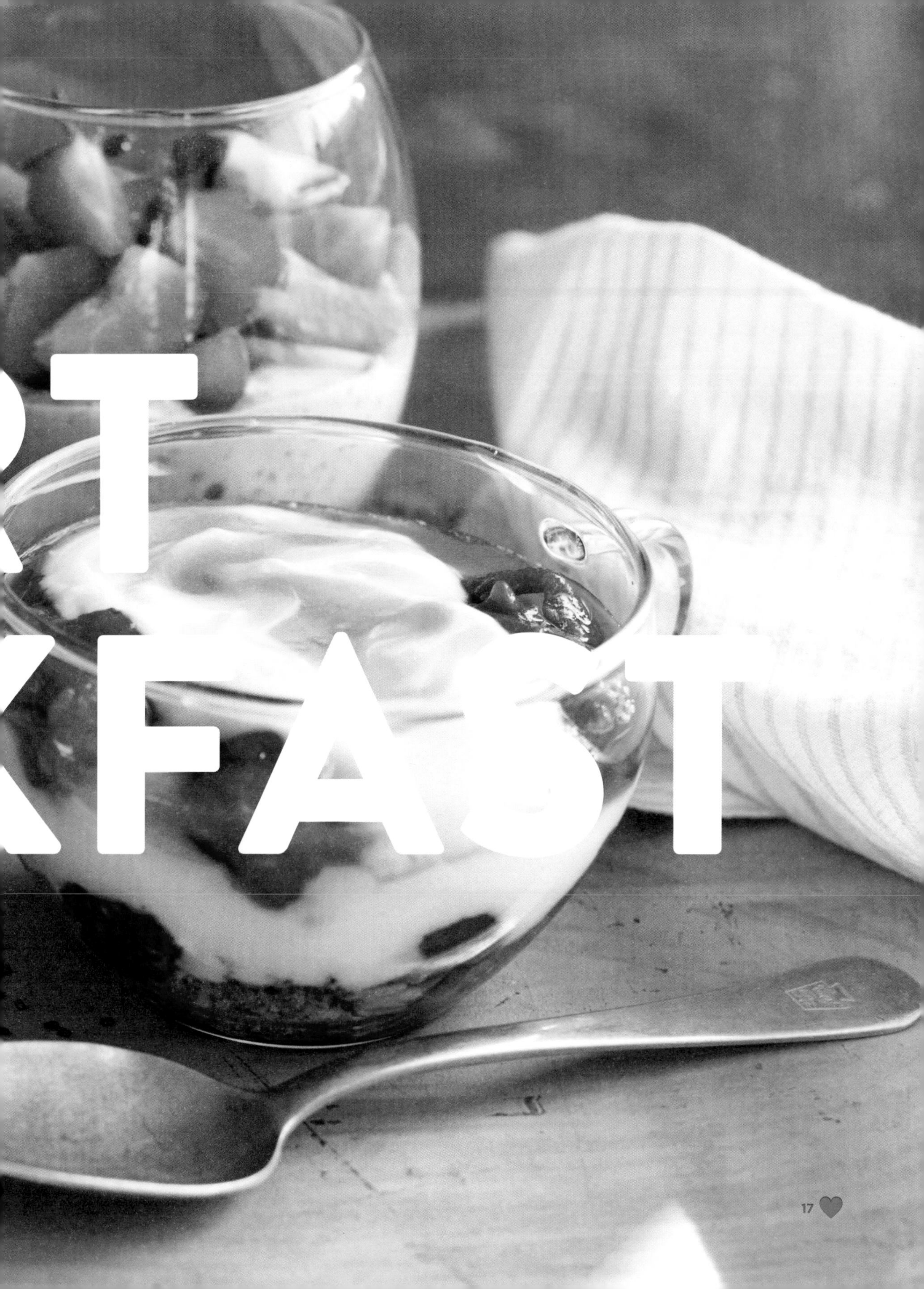
RT
KFAST

I heart breakfast. We're not all morning people. For many of us getting out of bed and into the shower is challenging enough, let alone preparing a tasty, nutritious breakfast.

But when it comes to looking after your heart, it's best to start as you mean to go on, and that means making your first meal of the day a healthy one.

In this chapter you'll find a selection of simple, delicious and nutritious recipes perfect for the weekday rush or a more leisurely Sunday brunch. Containing a healthy balance of ingredients, they'll help to keep you going until lunchtime, putting an end to mid-morning hunger pangs and the fatty and sugary snacks that can come with them.

And if you're not a morning person, or simply lack the time, why not dip your toe into the healthy breakfast habit by choosing something quick and simple, like a piece of fruit, a handful of nut and seed mix or a low-fat yoghurt, to start your day?

MANGO & ALMOND MILK DRINK

SERVES 2 **PREPARE** 5 MINS

1 mango (approx. 190g)

300ml unsweetened almond milk

1–2 tsp crunchy cashew butter

Zest and juice of a lime

 148 Kcal
619 kJ

This is the perfect start to any day. The mango provides a natural sweetness and exotic flavour, while the almond milk has hydrating qualities and the cashew butter packs a protein punch.

If you have a bit more time, try making your own Chunky Cashew Nut Butter | page 33 |.

Place all the ingredients, except the lime zest, into a liquidiser and blend until smooth.

Pour into two tall glasses filled with ice and serve topped with a scattering of the lime zest.

TRY ADDING YOUR OWN CRUNCHY
CASHEW NUT BUTTER (PAGE 33)

21

GOOD MORNING GREEN JUICE

SERVES 2 **PREPARE** 5 MINS

A couple of kale or spinach leaves, washed and any tough stalks removed (approx. 30g)

A handful of parsley (10g)

2 ripe kiwis, peeled and chopped

1 apple, such as Braeburn or Cox, cored and chopped

1 cm fresh root ginger, peeled and roughly chopped

Ice, to blitz and/or serve (optional)

Clear honey or agave nectar, to taste

90 Kcal
379 kJ

With vitamins and minerals like beta-carotene, vitamin C and potassium, this green energy juice is a refreshing pick-me-up for any morning.

Place all the ingredients except the ice and honey into a high-speed liquidiser with about 100ml of water. If your liquidiser is suitable for crushing ice, add a few cubes.

Pulse until smooth, then pour into glasses, over ice if you wish, and drink immediately, sweetened with honey or agave nectar to taste.

Note: Taste the juice before you add any honey or agave nectar. The natural sweetness will vary depending on the ripeness of the fruit and the time of year. Add the honey a little at a time and taste as you go to get the mix just right.

I also like to squeeze in a little fresh lime for extra flavour.

QUINOA PORRIDGE WITH BLUEBERRY COMPOTE

SERVES 2 **PREPARE** 5 MINS **COOK** 25 MINS

100g quinoa

300ml unsweetened almond milk or coconut-flavoured rice milk, plus extra to serve

200g fresh or frozen blueberries

Juice of ½ lemon

1–2 tsp chia seeds

1–2 tbsp agave nectar, date syrup or clear honey, to taste

To serve: Toasted flaked almonds, cinnamon, sliced fresh banana and extra blueberries

 414 Kcal
1730 kJ

Nutty in taste and filling by nature, quinoa is a versatile ingredient. A great source of protein, fibre and starchy carbohydrate, it's ideal for breakfast, especially if you're planning on doing some exercise later in the morning.

When cooked it becomes fluffy and creamy, making it a good alternative to oats for porridge. I like it flavoured with a pinch of cinnamon or nutmeg and a little date syrup.

Wash the quinoa in cold water, then pour into a fine sieve and drain well. Place in a small saucepan with 100ml cold water and the almond milk. Slowly bring to the boil and then reduce the heat to a gentle simmer. Stir frequently for 15 minutes, or until almost all the liquid has been absorbed and the quinoa is tender. Remove from the heat and allow to stand.

Meanwhile, place the blueberries in a small pan with the lemon juice and 50ml water, and simmer gently over a medium heat for 5–8 minutes or until the blueberries have burst and the compote has started to become jammy.

Stir the chia seeds into the porridge, then serve into 2 bowls, adding a splash of milk to loosen if needed.

Serve the porridge topped with a generous spoonful of the compote, the sliced banana and the toasted almonds. Sweeten to taste with the agave nectar, date syrup, honey or No-Cook Chia Berry Conserve | page 32 |.

Note: This also tastes great made with a mix of red and white quinoa and buckwheat.

Whether you use fresh or frozen blueberries, the amount in a portion of this recipe will still count as one of your five a day.

STRAWBERRY BIRCHER MUESLI

SERVES 2 **PREPARE** 5 MINS PLUS SOAKING

70g porridge oats

2 tsp chia seeds

150g low-fat natural yoghurt

100ml skimmed milk or
almond milk

Few drops of rose water

2 tbsp clear honey, agave nectar
or date syrup, plus extra to serve

200g strawberries, hulled
and sliced

322 Kcal
1346 kJ

Mornings can be a rush, so here's a deliciously simple breakfast
you can prepare the night before (and even munch on-the-go).
A new twist on traditional bircher, this strawberry bircher muesli
is a low-fat, high-fibre start to your day.

Stir together the oats and chia seeds. Add the yoghurt, milk,
rose water and honey and stir well. Divide between two tumblers
or jars – the mixture should fill the glasses by two-thirds. Cover
with cling film, or a lid, and chill overnight.

Divide the sliced strawberries between the glasses, drizzle
with a little extra honey and serve.

Note: Try adding a small handful of roasted hazelnuts, or sliced
bananas and blueberries, on top of each serving.

RASPBERRY & MUESLI BREAKFAST FOOL

SERVES 4 **PREPARE** 10 MINS PLUS CHILLING TIME **COOK** 5 MINS

250g fresh raspberries

6 tsp clear honey, agave nectar or date syrup

75g no added salt or sugar muesli

250g 0% fat Greek strained yoghurt

153 Kcal
646 kJ

At the heart of this assembly of ingredients is the mini-miracle that is 0% fat Greek strained yogurt. Wonderfully thick and creamy and yet completely fat-free, it makes for a filling choice and is a good source of protein to boot.

Place the raspberries (reserving a few for the garnish) with 2 tsp of the honey, agave nectar or date syrup and a teaspoon of water in a small saucepan and cook over a low heat until the fruit begins to soften. Remove from the heat and leave to cool slightly.

Spoon the muesli into four small serving glasses or jars and top with half the raspberry mix, followed by half the yoghurt. Add another layer of raspberries and a further layer of yoghurt.

Top each portion with the reserved raspberries and 1 tsp honey, agave nectar or date syrup drizzled over, and serve.

Note: Try adding toasted pumpkin seeds or chopped walnuts, pecans, goji berries or additional fresh raspberries.

BANANA & ALMOND SOAKED OATS

SERVES 2 **PREPARE** 5 MINS PLUS SOAKING

70g porridge oats

2 tsp chia seeds

1 ripe banana

2 tsp almond butter or homemade nut butter | page 33 |

150g low-fat natural yoghurt

100ml skimmed milk or almond milk

2 tbsp clear honey, agave nectar or date syrup, plus extra to serve

200g blueberries

To serve: Extra seasonal mixed berries, such as raspberries, blueberries and blackberries, and mixed unsalted seeds and nuts

444 Kcal
1856 kJ

This is a great choice for those who prefer an energy-fuelled breakfast. While the pre-soaked oats feel easy to digest, the well-balanced ingredients should keep you going all the way to lunch, or give you the oomph for a morning workout.

Stir together the oats and chia seeds, mash together the banana and almond nut butter and add to the oats.

Add the yoghurt, milk and honey and stir well. Divide between two tumblers or jars – the mixture should fill the glasses to two-thirds. Cover with cling film and chill overnight.

To serve, add more milk as needed to get the texture you like and then divide the blueberries between the glasses. Drizzle with a little extra honey, berries and a sprinkle of mixed seeds and nuts.

"There is no better taste to my mind than these banana & almond soaked oats. In addition, there's the satisfying knowledge that the components are definitely on the healthy side of tasty... not naughty, but nice."

SIR RANULPH FIENNES

STRAWBERRY BIRCHER MUESLI
(PAGE 26)

BANANA & ALMOND SOAKED OATS

RASPBERRY & MUESLI
BREAKFAST FOOL (PAGE 27)

29 ♥

SEEDED SODA BREAD

MAKES 1 LOAF (8–10 SLICES) **PREPARE** 10 MINS **COOK** 40 MINS

250g strong wholemeal bread flour, plus extra for dusting

200g wholegrain spelt flour

1 tsp salt

1 tsp bicarbonate of soda

300ml of buttermilk or natural yoghurt

1–2 tbsp sunflower seeds

173 Kcal
730 kJ

This easy-to-prepare soda bread is lovely served straight from the oven. Providing protein and fibre as well as starchy carbohydrate, spelt flour has a sweet, nutty flavour. The sunflower seeds provide a crunchy topping and are a good source of polyunsaturated fats, vitamins and minerals.

Preheat the oven to 200°C/gas mark 6. Place the flours in a large bowl and add the salt and bicarbonate of soda. Make a well in the centre, pour in the buttermilk, then, using a flat-sided knife, gently draw in the flour until combined. Bring the dough together with your hands and knead briefly on a lightly floured surface until smooth, adding a splash of water if needed.

Shape the dough into a ball and flatten slightly. Dust a baking sheet with wholemeal flour, place the loaf on top and scatter with the sunflower seeds.

Bake the soda bread in the oven for 40 minutes until loaf is risen, looks golden and sounds hollow when tapped.

Note: Using 450g spelt flour (omitting the wholemeal flour) also works for this recipe but gives a slightly dense loaf.

Try the soda bread toasted and topped with mashed avocado, a pinch of chilli flakes and a sprinkling of baby coriander leaves, or with some homemade No-Cook Chia Berry Conserve | page 32 |.

NO-COOK CHIA BERRY CONSERVE
(PAGE 32)

31

NO-COOK CHIA BERRY CONSERVE

SERVES 4 **PREPARE** 5 MINS PLUS SOAKING

2 tbsp chia seeds (20g)

4 tbsp coconut water

100g pack raspberries

50g pack blueberries

2 tbsp maple syrup

 73 Kcal
305 kJ

This chia berry jam is simple to make and works perfectly as a topping for the Oaty Drop Scones with Cranberries | page 37 | or the Seeded Soda Bread | page 30 |.

As well as containing vitamins and minerals from the berries, this jam contains protein and fibre from the chia seeds. Although they look small, the seeds swell to about nine times their size when added to liquid, giving this conserve the ideal consistency.

Place the chia seeds and coconut water in a tall container. Set aside to soak for 10 minutes until expanded. Add the raspberries, blueberries and the maple syrup to the container. Using a hand-held blender, whizz until well combined. The conserve can be stored in a jar in the fridge for 2–3 days.

Note: To enjoy this jam all year round, even when fresh berries aren't in season, simply defrost frozen berries instead.

This conserve is more than just a spread – try using it as a coulis for desserts, or spoon over homemade frozen yoghurt or low-fat natural yoghurt.

NUT BUTTER: 2 WAYS

CHUNKY CASHEW NUT BUTTER

MAKES APPROX. 15 TBSP (1 TBSP PER SERVING) **PREPARE** 15 MINS **COOK** 7–8 MINS

This is a great option for breakfast or a mid-morning snack. There's a bit of blending involved so you'll need a food processor. The trick is not to hurry, giving enough time for the nuts to turn into a satisfyingly smooth paste.

Spread over toasted rye bread or a rice cake and enjoy with a cup of fresh coffee – it's worth the wait and healthier than shop-bought.

350g cashew nuts
Pinch of cayenne pepper

Scatter the cashew nuts onto a non-stick baking sheet and roast at 180°C/gas mark 4 for 7–8 minutes until dark golden.

Leave to cool for a few minutes, then tip the nuts into a small food processor. Whizz until finely chopped.

Lift out a quarter of the nuts, then blend the remainder for 10 minutes to form a thick and creamy paste. Stir in the chopped nuts with a pinch of cayenne pepper. Scrape into a small airtight jar and store in the fridge for up to two weeks.

 88 Kcal
366 kJ

CINNAMON SPICED NUT BUTTER

MAKES APPROX. 12 TBSP (1 TBSP PER SERVING) **PREPARE** 15 MINS **COOK** 5–10 MINS

Just the thing if you have an energetic day ahead. Simply spread onto a toasted wholemeal muffin and top with a sliced banana for a filling breakfast. Or spread over apple slices for a nutritious snack – the subtle cinnamon flavour works a treat.

175g whole almonds, skin on
100g whole cashew nuts
½–1 tsp ground cinnamon (depending on taste)

Preheat the oven to 190°C/gas mark 5. Tip the nuts out onto two separate baking sheets. Roast the nuts for 5–10 minutes or until toasted - the cashews will need slightly less time than the almonds so take them out of the oven when done.

Leave the roasted nuts to cool slightly on the trays for 5 minutes.

Tip the warm nuts into a food processor and whizz until finely chopped. Add the cinnamon and continue to blend for about 10 minutes to form a smooth and creamy nut butter. Scrape into an airtight jar and store in the fridge for up to two weeks.

 144 Kcal
594 kJ

SIMON'S STORY

"BHF funding has helped researchers at the University of Cambridge develop a new ICD which can be implanted far more easily, helping prevent thousands of sudden cardiac arrests, like Simon's, every year."

– DR ANDREW DEANER
Cardiologist at London Chest Hospital

Dr Deaner helped save the life of retired professional footballer Fabrice Muamba, after he suffered a cardiac arrest on the pitch during an FA Cup match in 2012. Fabrice has since gone on to have a life-saving ICD fitted.

When I first met Simon, the words *'heart condition'* were the last that sprang to mind. Simon always enjoyed a healthy lifestyle, looking after himself with regular trips to the gym.

So it came as a bombshell, he told me, when at the age of just 24 he suffered a cardiac arrest in the middle of a weights session.

Luckily a personal trainer was on hand to administer cardiopulmonary resuscitation (CPR) and a defibrillator was used to return his heart to a normal rhythm.

Tests revealed Simon was living with a serious heart condition called dilated cardiomyopathy where the heart muscle becomes stretched, leaving it unable to pump blood efficiently around the body.

Although there is no cure for this condition, it is treatable, and Simon was fitted with an internal cardioverter defibrillator (ICD), a small device implanted in the chest that can detect if his heart goes into a dangerous rhythm and automatically correct it if needed.

Simon has learnt to live with the ICD and, with the help of tablets to lower his blood pressure, continues to enjoy a happy and healthy lifestyle with frequent workouts down at the gym.

OATY DROP SCONES WITH CRANBERRIES

MAKES 10 (1 PER SERVING) **PREPARE** 10 MINS **COOK** 20 MINS

50g porridge oats

250ml skimmed milk

175g wholemeal self-raising flour

1 tsp baking powder

½ tsp ground cinnamon (optional)

2 medium eggs

150g dried cranberries

Sunflower oil spray

94 Kcal
393 kJ

These oaty scones will make for a filling breakfast, cosy afternoon tea or weekend brunch. Serve with some No-Cook Chia Berry Conserve | page 32 | and a dollop of thick, low-fat Greek yoghurt for a healthier take on a cream tea.

Soak the oats in a little of the milk for 5 minutes. Mix together the flour, baking powder and cinnamon, if using. In a separate bowl, beat together the eggs and remaining milk. Make a well in the flour, pour in the liquid and beat together until smooth. Stir in the oat mixture and dried cranberries.

Spray a large non-stick frying pan or flat griddle with oil. Drop small, evenly-sized spoonfuls of the batter in the pan and cook for 1–2 minutes on each side until risen and golden brown. Check one to make sure they are cooked through. Serve warm with fresh berries and a tiny drizzle of clear honey.

Note: For a change, try swapping the dried cranberries for other dried fruits such as sultanas or raisins.

Any leftovers can be frozen and then toasted to warm them (and you) up another day.

EGGS ARE HIGH IN PROTEIN
AND SALMON IS A GOOD SOURCE
OF OMEGA-3 FATS

EGGS FLORENTINE

SERVES 4 **PREPARE** 10 MINS **COOK** 10 MINS

4 large eggs

400g bag fresh spinach,
roughly chopped

2 tbsp half-fat crème fraîche

1–2 tsp wholegrain mustard

2 wholemeal muffins, split
and toasted

4 slices of smoked salmon

To serve: 2 tbsp snipped chives

Saffron Yoghurt Aioli | page 226 |

235 Kcal
987 kJ

Not only is this dish a flavour-filled way to start the day, it's
quick to put together and full of nutrition.

Eggs are high in protein. Spinach comes with iron. Salmon is
a good source of omega-3 fats. And wholemeal muffins provide
us with starchy carbohydrates and fibre.

Bring a large pan of water to the boil. Crack an egg into a cup,
then gently tip into the boiling water. Repeat for the remaining
eggs, then remove from the heat and set aside for 5 minutes until
they're softly set.

Meanwhile, rinse the spinach and – with some of the water still
clinging to the leaves – place in a large saucepan. Cover with
a lid and cook gently for 2 minutes until wilted. Tip into a colander
and press to remove any excess liquid, then tip into a bowl and
mix in the crème fraîche and mustard. Spoon the mixture onto
the toasted muffins, then top each with smoked salmon.

Gently lift the eggs out of the hot water with a slotted spoon and
place on top of the smoked salmon slices. Sprinkle over the chives,
with a good grinding of black pepper, then serve swiftly with the
Saffron Yoghurt Aioli spooned over the top.

Note: Using half-fat crème fraîche for the sauce makes this a lighter,
healthier choice than traditional hollandaise, which is made with
melted butter.

ROCKET, BEANS & POACHED EGG ON TOAST

SERVES 4 **PREPARE** 10 MINS **COOK** 5 MINS

2 tbsp extra virgin olive oil

2 cloves garlic, finely sliced

1 bunch spring onions, finely sliced

½–1 tsp dried chilli flakes, to taste

400g can cannellini beans, drained and rinsed

100g rocket or watercress

4 slices rye, spelt or seeded bread, such as buckwheat & millet bread

4 eggs

292 Kcal
1222 kJ

Beans are a great source of fibre, making this dish a warming and nutritious start to the day. The rocket adds a peppery flavour and is a welcome change from the normal breakfast egg accompaniments.

Heat 1 tbsp of the oil in a frying pan and add the garlic, spring onions and chilli flakes. Cook over a high heat for 1–2 minutes, until golden.

Add the beans and heat through for 1–2 minutes. Add the rocket and cook for 30 seconds–1 minute, until it is starting to wilt, then set aside.

Bring a large pan of water to the boil. Crack an egg into a cup, gently tip into the boiling water and repeat with the remaining eggs. Remove from the heat and set aside for 5 minutes until softly set.

Meanwhile, toast the bread and drizzle with the remaining oil. Spoon over the beans and top with the poached egg.

TURKISH SCRAMBLED EGGS

SERVES 4 **PREPARE** 10 MINS **COOK** 15 MINS

1 tbsp olive oil

1 red onion, thinly sliced

1 clove garlic, finely chopped

1 red pepper, deseeded
and thinly sliced

4 spring onions, thinly sliced

¼ tsp cayenne pepper

2 tomatoes, quartered
and chopped

8 large eggs, beaten

A bunch of flat-leaf parsley,
chopped (25g)

40g light feta cheese

To serve: 4 wholemeal tortillas
or flat breads (optional)

214 Kcal
890 kJ

Here's a foreign twist on traditional scrambled eggs, inspired by the Mexican huevos rancheros. Packed with savoury ingredients, this Turkish version uses tomatoes, onions and red peppers to create a nourishing meal that will help you towards your five a day.

Heat 1 tbsp olive oil in a medium frying pan, then add the onion, garlic, pepper, spring onions and cayenne pepper. Cook for 8–10 minutes over a low heat until soft and golden.

Stir in the tomatoes and season. Cook over a high heat for 3–4 minutes until any moisture evaporates. Set aside and keep warm.

Beat the eggs together with the chopped parsley, then pour into the pan and stir over a medium heat for 1–2 minutes or until set to your liking. Stir in the reserved tomato and pepper mixture. Scatter with the feta and serve with warm tortillas or flatbreads.

MEDITERRANEAN HAM & TOMATOES ON TOAST

SERVES 2 **PREPARE** 5 MINS **COOK** 15–20 MINS

250g baby plum tomatoes, halved lengthways

A handful of chopped fresh basil (10g)

2 slices rye, spelt or seeded bread, such as buckwheat & millet bread

2 slices Serrano or Parma ham, or bresaola beef, with any visible fat removed

To serve: Tabasco sauce (optional)

145 Kcal
606 kJ

This is a simple, flavour-filled dish, especially when using tomatoes at their best and ripest. I like to make it with a five-minute boiled egg, peeled and served on the side.

Preheat the oven to 200°C/gas mark 6. Arrange the tomatoes, cut side up, in a shallow baking tray lined with baking parchment, and roast for 15–20 minutes. When they are very soft but just holding their shape, gently stir through half the basil.

Toast the bread, spoon the tomatoes over each slice, then tear the ham over the tomatoes. Season with black pepper, scatter over the remaining basil and add a splash of Tabasco, if you like, and serve.

Note: In addition to the basil, try roasting the tomatoes with a sprig of fresh thyme.

EGG & AVOCADO TORTILLA

SERVES 2 **PREPARE** 5 MINS **COOK** 5–7 MINS

2 wholemeal or seeded
tortilla wraps

½ ripe avocado, peeled
and stone removed

100g quark or low-fat
natural yoghurt

Squeeze of lemon

A handful of fresh coriander (10g)

2 medium eggs

To serve: Olive oil, finely
sliced red or green spring onions
and small green chillies

343 Kcal
1437 kJ

"I always love incorporating
avocado and egg into my
breakfast, it's one of my favourite
combinations. The wholewheat
tortilla also provides complex
carbohydrates and fibre which
are key when I'm training or have
a big day ahead of me."

LEWIS HAMILTON MBE

This is a tasty dish with a Latin American feel to it, especially with added green chillies.

The combination of starchy carbohydrate from the tortilla wrap and the protein from the yoghurt and eggs provides a healthy kickstart to the day. This dish is also a great refuelling snack after exercise.

Preheat the oven to 220°C/gas mark 7. Place each wrap on a baking sheet. Mash the avocado in a small bowl with the quark or yoghurt, a squeeze of lemon juice and coriander. Spread this avocado mix evenly over each wrap allowing a 1 cm border around the edge, with a slight hollow in the centre. Crack the egg in the centre and bake in the oven for 5–7 minutes, or until the egg is set and the yolk is the way you like it.

Remove from the oven, drizzle with the olive oil and season with freshly ground black pepper, then scatter with finely sliced spring onions and fresh green chilli, if liked.

Note: Try varying this recipe by topping with different combinations of seeds, dill, cucumber and Watercress Pesto | page 201 |.

SWEDISH TARTINE (OPEN SANDWICH)

SERVES 2 **PREPARE** 10 MINS **COOK** 2 MINS

1 medium egg

4 slices rye bread

100g thick 0% fat strained Greek yoghurt or skyr

2 tsp hot horseradish sauce

4 herrings, drained (from a jar of herrings in a dill marinade)

4 small cooked beetroots

5 cm piece of cucumber, diced

4 sprigs dill or cress

To serve: Thinly sliced red onion (optional)

335 Kcal
1480 kJ

This is one of my favourites. Not only do the herrings go beautifully with horseradish sauce and beetroot, but as an oily fish they also provide unsaturated omega-3 fatty acids which are recommended to help protect our heart health.

Enjoy. Or, as our friends in Sweden say, *smaklig måltid!*

Place the egg in a saucepan and completely cover with salted water. Bring to the boil, then reduce the heat and simmer gently for 7 minutes. Lift out the egg, tap it to crack the shell, then plunge into a bowl of iced water. Carefully peel the egg and cut into quarters.

Meanwhile, toast the rye bread. Mix together the yoghurt or skyr and horseradish sauce, then thickly spread on the toast and top with the herrings, sliced beetroot, diced cucumber and egg quarters. Season with a little black pepper, then garnish with the dill and red onion, if liked, and serve.

Note: If herring's not your thing, try using a similar quantity of hot smoked trout or salmon instead.

SPICY TOMATO & SPINACH BAKED EGGS

SERVES 2 **PREPARE** 10 MINS **COOK** 20-25 MINS

1 tsp olive oil

1 shallot, finely chopped

1 clove garlic, crushed

1 red pepper, deseeded and diced

Pinch of chilli flakes

400g can chopped tomatoes

1 tbsp tomato purée

200g baby spinach leaves

4 medium eggs

1 tbsp Parmigiano Reggiano,
finely grated

337 Kcal
1404 kJ

Not only is this spicy and warming dish ideal for a weekend brunch, it also provides more than two portions of your five a day thanks to the peppers, spinach and tomatoes.

Don't worry if the eggs spill over a little during cooking. They might end up looking like a giant fried egg but as long as you don't overcook them they'll taste great!

Preheat the oven to 200°C/gas mark 6. In a large saucepan, heat the olive oil and gently fry the shallot and garlic for 2–3 minutes, then add the pepper and cook for a further 2–3 minutes. Add the chilli flakes and cook for a minute more. Stir in the chopped tomatoes with the tomato purée and simmer for 3-4 minutes.

Stir in the spinach until just wilted and then spoon the mixture into two ovenproof dishes about 16 cm long (rectangular) or 17 cm (round). Make two dents in the sauce in each dish and crack in the eggs. Scatter with the Parmigiano Reggiano and season with freshly ground black pepper.

Place in the oven and bake for 12–14 minutes or until the egg whites have just set and the yolks are still soft. Serve with toasted sourdough or Seeded Soda Bread | page 30 | to soak up the juices.

STRAWBERRY BIRCHER
MUESLI | PAGE 26 |

GOOD BREAKFAST. GREAT DAY.

It really is true – a healthy breakfast will help stop you reaching out for sugary mid-morning snacks and will give you the energy you need for the morning ahead.

I heart on-the-go. We all lead busy lives. Unfortunately, healthy eating and hectic lifestyles don't always mix well.

When we're on-the-go it can be easier to grab something off-the-shelf, a ready-prepared meal that may be high in saturated fat, salt and sugar.

But with a bit of planning we can help Hectic and Healthy become the best of friends.

The recipes in this chapter offer a selection of tasty salads and snacks that you can pack up and take with you.

Here's to the beginning of a beautiful friendship.

FIERY RED PEPPER SOUP

SERVES 4   **PREPARE** 10 MINS   **COOK** 60 MINS

4–5 red peppers, quartered and deseeded

50g large red chillies, halved and deseeded

4 carrots, cut into chunks

Olive oil spray

1.5 litres hot, homemade vegetable stock | page 15 | or ready-made, low-salt alternative

75–100g red lentils

To serve: 4 tsp reduced-fat soured cream

3 tbsp toasted mixed seeds (50g)

250 Kcal
1046 kJ

This is a hearty soup, thickened with red lentils for extra protein and fibre. The chilli gives a warming kick that is softened by the sweetness of the red peppers – a really satisfying and nourishing combination.

Preheat the oven to 200°C/gas mark 6. Place the peppers, chillies and carrots in a large roasting tin and spritz with the olive oil spray. Roast for 50–60 minutes, until all the vegetables are tender.

Meanwhile, place the heated stock and lentils in a large pan. Cover and simmer for 30 minutes or so, until the lentils are soft, then tip the vegetables (reserving one of the roast pepper quarters for the garnish) and their juices into the pan. Using a hand-held blender, whizz the soup until smooth.

Ladle into bowls and swirl in a teaspoon of reduced-fat soured cream, finely slice the reserved pepper, and arrange a little of the sliced pepper on each soup before scattering over the seeds and serving with the Seeded Soda Bread | page 30 |.

WATERCRESS & PEA SOUP

SERVES 4 **PREPARE** 5 MINS **COOK** 10 MINS

1 tsp olive oil

1 small leek, washed and finely chopped

2 cloves garlic, crushed

750ml homemade vegetable stock | page 15 | or ready-made, low-salt alternative

100g watercress

100g spinach

A bunch of flat-leaf parsley (25g)

400g fresh or frozen peas

To serve: 4 tsp low-fat natural yoghurt (about 30g)

108 Kcal
453 kJ

The peppery flavour of the watercress in this soup is really tasty when combined with the sweetness of the peas.

I love the versatility of watercress. It can be used as a salad leaf to give a peppery kick or as the star ingredient, like in this thick and wholesome green soup. I can't get enough of it!

Heat the oil in the base of a large, deep saucepan and fry the leek and garlic for 3–4 minutes, stirring occasionally, until the leek starts to soften. Add the stock and bring to the boil.

Save four small sprigs of parsley for a garnish and place the watercress, spinach and remaining flat-leaf parsley with the peas in the soup, return to the boil and cook for 2–3 minutes until it begins to wilt but still retains its colour. Season with cracked black pepper, then blend until smooth using an electric hand blender or food processor.

Ladle the warm or chilled soup into individual bowls and top with a spoonful of natural yoghurt (if liked) and the reserved parsley.

Note: If you like, try sprinkling with some toasted pumpkin seeds and a dusting of chilli flakes, too.

SOBA NOODLES, CHICKEN & GINGER SOUP

SERVES 2 **PREPARE** 10 MINS **COOK** 20 MINS

500ml homemade chicken stock | page 15 | or ready-made, low-salt alternative

½ onion, thinly sliced

1 clove garlic, thinly sliced

3 cm piece fresh root ginger, grated, plus extra for garnish

½ red chilli, sliced, plus extra for garnish

2 tsp low-salt soy sauce

100g buckwheat soba noodles

4 shiitake mushrooms, thinly sliced

100g beansprouts

2 spring onions, sliced

1 chicken breast, very thinly sliced

To serve: Fresh coriander, chilli and ginger

327 Kcal
1367 kJ

This feels light and cleansing – perfect as a lunch or starter for those times when you don't want to be weighed down by a heavy meal.

It's quick to prepare and full of flavour from the chilli, garlic and coriander, which means you don't need to add as much salt as you'd normally find in this type of dish.

Pour the stock into a large saucepan and add the onion, garlic, ginger, chilli and soy sauce. Simmer gently for about 10 minutes, or until the onions are soft and translucent.

Meanwhile, place the noodles in a pan of boiling water and bring to the boil, simmer for 5 minutes, drain and rinse under cold water.

Strain stock to remove onion, garlic, ginger and chilli, if you wish. Stir the remaining ingredients with 100ml boiling water into the stock. Return to the boil, then reduce to a simmer and leave covered for a further 5–10 minutes until the chicken is cooked and there is no pink meat. Stir in the cooked noodles and return to the boil.

Garnish with fresh coriander, finely sliced chilli and fresh ginger.

Note: You can also try this with fresh jumbo prawns and more green veg – try baby spinach leaves or some small pak choi leaves dropped into the broth with the other ingredients at the end of cooking.

"I'm a big fan of Japanese food for its simplicity and cleanliness. A chicken noodle soup was a staple diet for me as an athlete."

ROGER BLACK MBE

PEA & SWEET POTATO SAMOSAS

MAKES 12 (3 PER SERVING) **PREPARE** 15 MINS PLUS COOLING **COOK** 25 MINS

250g sweet potatoes, diced

100g frozen petits pois, thawed

4 spring onions, thinly sliced

1 tsp garam masala

½ tsp cumin seeds, toasted

Pinch of crushed chilli flakes

4 sheets filo pastry

Sunflower oil spray

 304 Kcal
1271 kJ

These spiced vegetable samosas are made with filo pastry and baked rather than fried, which makes them much healthier than traditional samosas.

They can be eaten hot or cold and make a tasty on-the-go snack or, if you fold them a little smaller, perfect canapés. I love them with a dip, too – try raita or the Roasted Cucumber Tzatziki | page 67 |.

Cook the sweet potatoes in a pan of boiling water for 10 minutes until tender. Drain, mash lightly and mix in the peas, spring onions, garam masala, cumin and chilli flakes. Cover and leave to cool.

Preheat the oven to 180°C/gas mark 4. Cut each sheet of filo into three long strips and spray lightly with sunflower oil. Place a tablespoon of the mixture just off centre at the end of one of the strips and fold over the corner to form a triangle shape. Keep folding the pastry, maintaining a triangle shape until you get to the end. Dampen with a little water to seal the end. Repeat with the remaining pastry and filling.

Transfer to a baking sheet, spritz with oil and bake for 10–15 minutes until golden. Serve warm with a salad.

Note: These are always handy to have in the freezer. Just assemble the samosas without baking them, then freeze in an airtight container. When you're ready to use them, take out the samosas you need, allow to thaw and bake as instructed.

BEETROOT FALAFELS WITH A YOGHURT DRESSING

MAKES 20 (5 PER SERVING) **PREPARE** 25 MINS **COOK** 10 MINS

400g can chickpeas, drained and rinsed

150g fresh beetroot, trimmed, scrubbed, peeled and grated

2 cloves garlic, crushed

50g plain flour

1 tsp ground coriander

1–2 tsp dried chilli flakes (optional)

Zest and juice of 1 lemon

2 tbsp olive oil, to fry

To serve: 100ml natural low-fat yoghurt mixed with tahini, Roasted Cucumber Tzatziki | page 67 | or Homemade Houmous | page 73 |

Rocket

Warm wholemeal flatbreads or pitta bread

1 red onion, finely sliced (optional – see note)

Approx. 200g poached salmon (optional)

426 Kcal
1781 kJ

This is a great dish to make the most of beetroot season, when the veg are sweet and full of flavour. Beetroots are rich in nitrates, which have been linked to beneficial effects on blood pressure. I use purple beets here to add a vibrant twist to this traditional Middle Eastern dish.

Blitz the chickpeas in a food processor. Then add the beetroot, garlic, flour, coriander, chilli flakes (if using) and lemon zest. Blitz to a rough paste – it should not be too smooth – then with damp hands roll into about 20 walnut-sized balls (falafels) and chill until ready to cook.

Add 1 tbsp olive oil to a non-stick frying pan and gently fry half the falafels for 5 minutes, turning frequently until crisp on each side. Remove and keep warm in the oven while the other batch is fried.

Serve the falafels with the red onions, yoghurt, tzatziki or houmous, the salmon (if liked), rocket and warm flatbreads or pittas.

Note: If you wish, steep the onion in the lemon juice and leave for about 20 minutes to colour and soften the flavour.

If you don't need all the falafels, they freeze well at the point where you've just rolled them into balls, so you can keep them for another day. Then simply let them defrost in the fridge and pan-fry them, following the rest of the recipe.

MINT & PEA FALAFELS
(PAGE 66)

PEA & SWEET POTATO
SAMOSAS (PAGE 62)

ROASTED CUCUMBER
TZATZIKI (PAGE 67)

BEETROOT FALAFELS
(PAGE 63)

MINT & PEA FALAFELS

MAKES 20 (5 PER SERVING) **PREPARE** 25 MINS **COOK** 10 MINS

150g frozen peas, thawed

115g baby spinach

A bunch of mint leaves, stalks discarded (25g)

400g can chickpeas, drained and rinsed

3 cloves garlic, crushed

50g plain flour

2 tsp ground cumin

2 tbsp chopped chives

¼ tsp chilli flakes

1 red onion, finely sliced

Juice and zest of 1 lemon

2 tbsp olive oil

To serve: 4 pitta breads

Natural low-fat yoghurt mixed with tahini or Homemade Houmous | page 73 |

Chopped pistachios

Rocket

Lemon wedges

397 Kcal
1670 kJ

It's not just chickpeas that make good falafels – you can experiment with a range of peas, beans and lentils, adding different herbs and spices for alternative flavour combinations.

Rather than deep-frying, which is the traditional way of cooking these patties, I find they're just as good cooked in only a little bit of oil. You still get that lovely, crispy outside but with a lot less fat. These are nice as a lunch or a mini canapé, especially dipped into raita or Roasted Cucumber Tzatziki | page 67 |.

Cook the peas for 2 minutes in boiling water, drain, then cool under fresh cold water. Set aside. Place the spinach and mint leaves in a colander, pour over a kettleful of boiling water to wilt and then run under cold water to refresh. Squeeze out the excess moisture with your hands. Chop and set aside.

Place the peas, spinach, mint, chickpeas, garlic, flour, cumin, chives, chilli flakes and some seasoning in a food processor and blitz to a rough paste. If it is too sticky, add some more flour. With damp hands, roll the mixture into about 20 walnut-sized balls. Place on a large plate, cover and chill until ready to cook. You can do this up to 4 hours ahead.

Mix the onion and lemon juice together and leave for 20 minutes to soften their flavour. Warm 1 tbsp of the olive oil in a large frying pan over a medium heat. Fry half of the falafels for 5 minutes, turning frequently, until golden on each side. Remove and keep warm in the oven, while you cook the next batch in the remaining oil.

Heat a griddle or frying pan and warm the pitta breads for about 1–2 minutes, turning occasionally. Serve the falafels with the warm pittas, red onions, yoghurt or houmous, a rocket salad and lemon wedges. Sprinkle with chopped pistachios.

ROASTED CUCUMBER TZATZIKI

SERVES 4–6 **PREPARE** 15 MINS **COOK** 20 MINS

2 large cucumbers, halved, deseeded and cut into 0.5 cm thick slices

2 tbsp olive oil

300g low-fat Greek yoghurt

2 tsp capers in brine, drained and roughly chopped

1 clove garlic, crushed

2 tbsp chopped dill

2 tbsp shredded mint leaves

Juice of ½ lemon

84 Kcal
351 kJ

Roasting cucumbers may sound strange but it makes such a difference to their flavour. This tasty dip can be enjoyed with cold meats, Wholegrain Chicken Shawarma | page 78 |, Mint & Pea Falafels | page 66 | or Pea & Sweet Potato Samosas | page 62 |.

Preheat the oven to 200°C/gas mark 6. Toss the sliced cucumber in the oil, season and spread out in a single layer on a large, foil-lined baking tray. Roast for 15–20 minutes until just turning golden at the edges. Set aside to cool.

Mix the yoghurt with 2 tbsp water to loosen it. Stir in the remaining ingredients, then toss with the roasted cucumber. Season and serve.

SMOKED HAM & SWEET POTATO TORTILLA

SERVES 4 **PREPARE** 20 MINS **COOK** 35 MINS

500g sweet potatoes, peeled
and cut into 1 cm cubes

2 tbsp light olive oil

1 large onion, finely sliced

6 large eggs

¼ tsp sweet smoked paprika

A handful of fresh flat-leaf parsley,
finely chopped (10g)

100g smoked ham, sliced
into small pieces

110g chargrilled peppers,
from a jar, drained and chopped

380 Kcal
1588 kJ

I really like the Spanish flavours in this tortilla. Packed with vegetables, it's a meal in a pan, making it tasty and satisfying any time of the day. This dish is equally good hot or cold so you could make it for dinner one night, and then take any leftovers to work for lunch the next day.

Preheat the oven to 190°C/gas mark 5. Toss the sweet potato cubes in 1 tbsp olive oil and then arrange in a single layer over a roasting tray. Roast for 25–30 minutes, until tender.

Preheat the grill to its highest setting. Heat the remaining oil in a 24 cm non-stick frying pan and gently fry the onion for 4–5 minutes, until golden and soft.

Whisk the eggs lightly together in a jug with the smoked paprika and parsley.

Add the roasted sweet potato cubes to the softened onions, followed by the ham, peppers and a little seasoning.

Pour the egg mixture over, moving the ingredients around with a fork before leaving to gently cook over a medium heat for about 10 minutes until the egg is just set.

Finish cooking the tortilla under the grill for 2–3 minutes until golden. If serving cold, leave to stand in the pan before cutting into wedges. Serve with some salad leaves.

CAROLINE'S STORY

It was a privilege to spend time with Caroline and hear her story. It began back in 2008 when her father was diagnosed with something called arrhythmogenic right ventricular cardiomyopathy (ARVC), an inherited condition that affects the heart muscle.

As a result the whole family were tested and it was found that Caroline also carried the faulty gene.

Having supported her father as he underwent treatment for ARVC, including the fitting of an internal cardioverter defibrillator (ICD), Caroline found it was now the turn of her husband Rob to support her as she came to terms with the news.

Recently married and wanting a family of their own, the couple were painfully aware that the faulty gene could be passed down to their own children. However, in 2014, after counselling and much deliberation, they became the proud parents of a healthy baby girl, Zara.

Today, apart from avoiding more strenuous sports and activities, Caroline is still able to live a happy and healthy life with her family.

Both she and her daughter have regular check-ups and I'm happy to say the results have been promising, with no symptoms detected.

In the future Zara can be tested for the faulty gene, but her parents have decided that will be only when she's old enough to understand the implications. Whatever the result, one thing is certain, she will have the love and support of two very special parents.

BABA GANOUSH (AUBERGINE DIP)

SERVES 2 **PREPARE** 10 MINS PLUS COOLING & DRAINING **COOK** 15–20 MINS

1 aubergine

1 clove garlic, crushed

Juice of ½ a lemon

1 tbsp tahini

2 heaped tbsp low-fat natural yoghurt (optional)

½ tsp sumac spice

1 tbsp chopped flat-leaf parsley

1 tbsp pomegranate seeds

To serve: 2 wholemeal pitta breads, toasted and cut into strips

½ cucumber, cut into fingers

2 carrots, peeled and cut into sticks

Extra virgin olive oil

136 Kcal
565 kJ

This is really easy to make and useful to have in the fridge to add to dishes. It's just as versatile as houmous, too. Spread it thickly on rye toast and top with griddled courgette strips, use instead of guacamole in fajitas, or serve with the Lamb with Roasted Cumin Cauliflower | page 176 |.

The tahini, lemon and sumac add classic Middle Eastern flavours to this dish, but use the sumac sparingly to keep the salt content down.

Preheat the grill to high. Prick the aubergine with a fork and grill, turning occasionally, until the skin blisters and blackens all over, for about 15–20 minutes or until the flesh is very soft (otherwise it will be difficult to purée). Once cool, peel, discard the skin and roughly chop. Place the aubergine flesh in a colander for 15 minutes to drain off excess liquid. Season with black pepper.

Transfer to a food processor. Add the garlic, lemon juice, tahini and yoghurt, if using. Whizz to a thick purée. Adjust the seasoning. Transfer to a bowl, drizzle with oil, sprinkle with sumac, parsley and pomegranate seeds and serve with a selection of toasted pitta breads, carrot and cucumber sticks.

HOUMOUS & VEGGIE WRAPS

HOMEMADE HOUMOUS

SERVES 4–6 **PREPARE** 10 MINS

Houmous is not just a humble dip. There are so many things you can do with a batch, from serving a generous spoonful with some lean roast lamb and Mediterranean vegetable wraps to spreading on rice cakes or cucumber with paprika as part of an antipasti platter.

400g can chickpeas, drained and rinsed
4 tbsp tahini (about 80g)
2 cloves garlic, crushed
Juice of 1 lemon
3 tbsp extra virgin olive oil (plus extra to serve)
To serve: Smoked paprika and pine nuts

Place the chickpeas, tahini, garlic and lemon juice in a food processor and blend until smooth. With the motor running, drizzle in the olive oil to form a smooth cream, adding a little extra if needed to get the desired consistency. Season. Transfer to a bowl and cover, then chill until ready to serve.

Serve sprinkled with a pinch of paprika, pine nuts and a small drizzle of olive oil, if you wish, with vegetable crudités and strips of toasted wholemeal pitta bread.

187 Kcal
774 kJ

HOUMOUS & VEGGIE WRAPS

SERVES 2 **PREPARE** 10 MINS **COOK** 4 MINS

These wraps make a satisfying veggie lunch, plump with lots of tasty filling. Wholegrain wraps have more fibre than standard white ones and the other ingredients will help you towards your five a day, too.

2 wholemeal wraps
4 tbsp houmous (see left)
½ ripe avocado, peeled and stone removed
25g baby spinach
1 plum tomato, diced
4 cm piece cucumber, diced
Squeeze of lemon
To serve: 2 tsp mixed seeds, toasted
A pinch of chilli flakes

Warm a ridged grill pan or non-stick frying pan over a medium heat. Warm each wrap for a minute on each side, then place on a board. Generously spread half of the houmous over the surface of each. Slice the avocado over the top, scatter over the spinach, diced tomato and cucumber and squeeze the lemon over. Sprinkle over the toasted seeds, chilli flakes, season with black pepper, then roll up and wrap in baking parchment until ready to serve.

Note: Other delicious additions are fresh herbs, spices, pomegranate seeds, fresh chilli and a drizzle of garlic or chilli-infused oil.

421 Kcal
1761 kJ

KALE & TUNA NIÇOISE SALAD

SERVES 2 **PREPARE** 5 MINS **COOK** 10 MINS

2 tbsp olive oil

1 tbsp balsamic vinegar

200g kale

2 medium eggs

Vegetable oil spray

150g tuna steak

Crushed pink peppercorns,
to taste

250g bunched asparagus,
trimmed

120g red and yellow cherry
tomatoes, halved

30g pitted black olives, sliced

1 green chilli

Tabasco sauce (optional)

355 Kcal
1475 kJ

Fresh, colourful and tasty, kale makes a nice change from the usual niçoise salad ingredients. This dark, leafy green vegetable is full of flavour and rich in a variety of nutrients.

Olives add a salty element, but by balancing out a small amount with plenty of veg you can enjoy the flavour – a little goes a long way.

In a large bowl, whisk together the olive oil and vinegar with a little freshly ground black pepper and set aside. Cook the kale in boiling water for 3–4 minutes, plunge into cold water, then drain thoroughly. Discard any thick stalks. Toss into the oil and vinegar dressing.

Meanwhile, place the eggs in a pan of cold water and bring to the boil. Simmer for 5–10 minutes (depending on your choice of soft or hard-boiled egg), then cool in cold water and peel.

Heat a non-stick frying pan, spray the tuna with a little vegetable oil and season with the pink peppercorns, then pan-fry for 2–3 minutes on each side, according to taste.

Slice the asparagus into 2.5 cm pieces. Steam or boil for 2 minutes, then rinse in cold water. Cut the eggs into quarters and slice the tuna steak. Divide the kale into 2 bowls and top with the asparagus, tomatoes, egg, olives, chilli and tuna and season to taste with Tabasco, if using.

Note: Kale leaves are quite coarse compared to other salad leaves and so benefit from light cooking. Alternatively, massage the shredded raw leaves in a little unsaturated oil.

You can also sprinkle with toasted sesame seeds to garnish.

TUSCAN BEAN PASTA SALAD

SERVES 2 **PREPARE** 15 MINS **COOK** 45–55 MINS

200g cherry tomatoes, halved,
at room temperature

2 romano peppers

2 tsp sherry vinegar

1 clove garlic, roughly chopped

1½ tbsp extra virgin olive oil

Pinch of sugar

Juice ½ lemon

200g wholewheat fusilli pasta

100g mixed pitted olives,
roughly chopped

150g chargrilled artichoke hearts
in olive oil, drained (optional)

A handful of fresh chives,
roughly chopped (10g)

A handful of basil, leaves
roughly torn (10g)

2 handfuls of rocket,
roughly chopped (40g)

½ × 400g can beans such as
mixed beans or borlotti beans,
drained and rinsed

639 Kcal
2671 kJ

Here's a really filling and robust salad with lots of flavour. It's a great choice to pack into a lunchbox on an active day, as it'll keep you going right through the afternoon. The lack of lettuce leaves means that, unlike more delicate salads, this one can withstand being bashed around a bit in your bag!

Preheat the oven to 150°C/gas mark 2. Place the cherry tomatoes in a roasting tin and cook in the oven for 45 minutes, until slightly caramelised.

Preheat the grill to high. Place the whole peppers in the grill pan and cook for 10 minutes, turning frequently, until blackened and charred. Remove from the heat, place in a bowl and cover with cling film until cool enough to handle. Carefully rub off most of the blackened skin, then slit the peppers open with a knife and remove the seeds and stalks.

Place the pepper flesh in a small food processor with the vinegar, garlic, olive oil, sugar and lemon juice. Blitz until smooth, season and set aside.

Cook the pasta in a large pan of boiling water for 10 minutes or until al dente. Drain well and toss in a large bowl with the dressing until coated, then leave to cool to room temperature.

Mix in the olives, artichokes, herbs, rocket, roasted tomatoes and beans, then serve.

WHOLEGRAIN CHICKEN SHAWARMA

SERVES 2 **PREPARE** 20–25 MINS PLUS MARINATING **COOK** 15–18 MINS

2 skinless, boneless chicken breasts

For the marinade:

1 onion, roughly chopped

2 tsp baharat spice blend

2 cloves garlic, crushed

Grated zest and juice of 1 lemon

1 tbsp extra virgin olive oil

To serve: 2 wholemeal flatbreads or wraps

2–3 tbsp Saffron Yoghurt Aioli | page 226 | or low-fat natural yoghurt

A handful of lettuce leaves

1 large tomato, very thinly sliced

5 cm piece of cucumber, sliced

½ red onion, very thinly sliced

Squeeze of lemon juice

441 Kcal
1843 kJ

These chicken kebabs are full of flavour and make a great packed lunch. Baharat is a blend of spices including cumin, coriander, black pepper, cinnamon, cardamom and cloves – you can find it in bigger supermarkets or Middle Eastern shops. It adds a wonderful flavour and, unlike many other spice mixes, doesn't have added salt, which makes it a healthier option for your heart.

To make the marinade, place the onion in a food processor and whizz in bursts until very finely chopped or puréed. Tip the onion onto a piece of muslin, pull the corners together and squeeze into a large bowl to extract the onion juice. Alternatively, strain with a fine sieve to remove the juice.

Place the pulp into a bowl and mix in the baharat, garlic, lemon zest, juice and olive oil. Season, then add the chicken, rubbing the marinade in well. Cover and place in the fridge to marinate for 15–20 minutes, or overnight if you have time.

Preheat a griddle pan over a high heat. Remove the chicken from the marinade and dry with some clean kitchen paper. Place the chicken on the griddle and cook for 15–18 minutes, turning occasionally, until lightly charred and firm to the touch, or until thoroughly cooked with no pink meat and the juices running clear.

Place the chicken on a chopping board, allow to rest for 2–3 minutes, then slice into strips. To serve, place each flatbread or wrap on a plate, spread with the Saffron Yoghurt Aioli and top with lettuce, tomato, cucumber, sliced chicken and onion. Season with additional baharat spice, if liked, then squeeze over some lemon juice, roll up and serve.

BAHARAT DOESN'T HAVE ADDED
SALT WHICH MAKES IT A HEALTHIER
OPTION FOR YOUR HEART

LOVE YOUR FRUIT AND VEG

Eating at least five portions of fruit and veg a day is linked to a lower risk of coronary heart disease and stroke, so try to get in the habit of making them a big part of every meal.

GRIDDLED MACKEREL & BEETROOT LENTIL SALAD

SERVES 4 **PREPARE** 15 MINS **COOK** 25–30 MINS

200g puy lentils

800ml homemade vegetable
stock | page 15 | or ready-
made, low-salt alternative

8 fresh mackerel fillets
(each fillet about 70g)

Finely grated zest and juice
of 1 lemon

150g beetroot, trimmed and grated

A bunch of flat-leaf parsley,
chopped (25g)

A bunch of dill, chopped (25g)

1 small red onion, finely chopped

1 tbsp sherry vinegar

½ tsp chilli flakes (optional)

½ tsp sumac

505 Kcal
2111 kJ

This salad makes a lovely light lunch, particularly if you can get hold
of really fresh mackerel. The mackerel goes perfectly with the
beetroot and lentils, but you could replace it with any other oily fish,
such as sardines or trout – all are sources of omega-3 fats.

Place the lentils with the vegetable stock in a saucepan, bring to
the boil, then simmer for 25–30 minutes, or until the lentils are just
tender. Drain thoroughly and tip into a bowl.

Lay the mackerel fillets in a shallow dish, pour over the lemon juice
and sprinkle with the lemon zest, and leave to marinade for about
5 minutes.

Stir the grated beetroot, parsley, dill and onion into the bowl of
lentils with the vinegar and chilli flakes, then set aside.

Heat a large griddle pan or non-stick frying pan over a high heat
and cook the mackerel for 2 minutes on each side, or until cooked
through – you might need to do this in batches.

To serve, spoon the lentil salad onto plates and top with the griddled
mackerel fillets sprinkled with sumac and a wedge of lemon on the
side, if you wish.

VIETNAMESE-STYLE PRAWN SPRING ROLLS

MAKES 6 **PREPARE** 25 MINS

1 nest vermicelli rice noodles

6 rice paper spring roll wrappers

12 cooked king prawns,
halved lengthways

2 handfuls of round lettuce, torn
into leaves (35g)

Large handful fresh mint leaves

Large handful fresh coriander

Large handful chives

1 small carrot, grated,
shredded or thinly sliced

To serve: 4 tbsp sweet chilli
dipping sauce (optional)

197 Kcal
823 kJ

These are one of my favourite snacks, easily packed into a container for lunch on-the-go. Although there's no bread, they're still really satisfying and filling. Enjoy three or four as a portion for lunch.

Put the noodles in a bowl of just-boiled water, cover and leave to soften for 5 minutes, then drain and rinse under cold water. Spread out to dry on kitchen paper and set aside.

Fill a large bowl with warm water. Submerge a spring roll wrapper in the water for 2 seconds and then place flat on a clean, dry plate. Don't worry if it still seems tough, the wrappers will continue to soften.

Place 4 prawn halves along the centre of the rice paper and top with some noodles, lettuce, herbs and carrots, making sure not to overfill and to leave room at the sides.

Fold the bottom of the rice paper completely over the filling, and then fold in the sides and roll up as tightly as possible. Repeat with the remaining sheets of rice paper and filling and serve with the dipping sauce, if you wish.

Note: Make one roll at a time, soaking each wrapper as you go to avoid them becoming too soggy.

You can also replace the prawns with 125g fresh crab meat.

ENERGY BALLS

MAKES 20 (1 PER SERVING) **PREPARE** 10 MINS

75g whole almonds,
roughly chopped

250g soft dates,
roughly chopped

A pinch of chilli flakes
(optional)

25g golden linseeds

 47 Kcal
197 kJ

These are quick and easy to make in a food processor, and packed with nutritious energy. They're a great snack to have in your bag for those days when you don't have much time for lunch, or need an energy boost after exercising. More importantly, they stop you reaching out for the chocolate!

Place the nuts in a food processor and blitz until finely chopped, then add the soft dried dates, and chilli flakes, if using. Continue to blitz in the food processor for a further 2–4 minutes or until the mixture has formed a thick smooth paste which has incorporated the nuts.

Divide the fruit and nut paste into 20×15g pieces, using wet hands to roll into round balls, and place on a tray lined with baking parchment paper. Roll the date and almond balls in the linseeds and store in an airtight container.

POPPED CORN: 2 WAYS

SPICED POPPED CORN & KALE CRISPS

SERVES 6 **PREPARE** 2 MINS **COOK** 20 MINS

For the kale crisps:
200g kale, shredded and large stalks removed
1 tbsp olive oil

For the popcorn:
2 tsp vegetable oil
100g popcorn maize
2 tsp smoked paprika
½–1 tsp mild chilli powder
Zest of 1 lime

For guilt-free snacking, try this spiced popcorn with kale crisps. By making your own, you can avoid the added salt and sugar that come with most popcorn you buy in the shops. Great to serve as nibbles too, when entertaining.

Preheat the oven to 200°C/gas mark 6. Toss the kale leaves with the oil and spread out over two large baking sheets lined with baking parchment. Bake for 12–15 minutes until crisp. Tip into a large bowl to cool.

Meanwhile, pour the vegetable oil into a large wide saucepan and place over the heat for 1–2 minutes or until hot. Sprinkle in the popcorn maize, cover with a lid, turn the heat down low and listen for the sound of the corn popping. Shake the pan frequently and leave on the heat until the popping subsides. Then toss the popcorn into the bowl with the kale, mix with the spices and lime zest and serve straight away.

91 Kcal
379 kJ

FRUIT & NUT POPPED CORN

SERVES 6 **PREPARE** 2 MINS **COOK** 3–5 MINS

2 tsp vegetable oil
100g popcorn maize
1 tsp ground cinnamon
75g sultanas
100g pecans, toasted

This is a moreish snack that I could eat any time of the day. This version combines sweet and savoury – the sweet element is a far cry from sugary-coated popcorn – and has a pleasing crunch factor.

Pour the vegetable oil into a large wide saucepan and place over the heat for 1–2 minutes or until hot. Sprinkle in the popcorn maize, cover with a lid, turn the heat down low and listen for the sound of the corn popping. Shake the pan frequently and leave on the heat until the popping subsides. Toss the popcorn with the remaining ingredients and serve straight away.

Note: Try adding chopped candied orange peel or any other dried fruit and toasted nut combinations. I like cranberries and hazelnuts or goji berries and walnuts.

Store either popped corn in an airtight container to munch through over a few days.

251 Kcal
1042 kJ

I HEAR

FAMIL

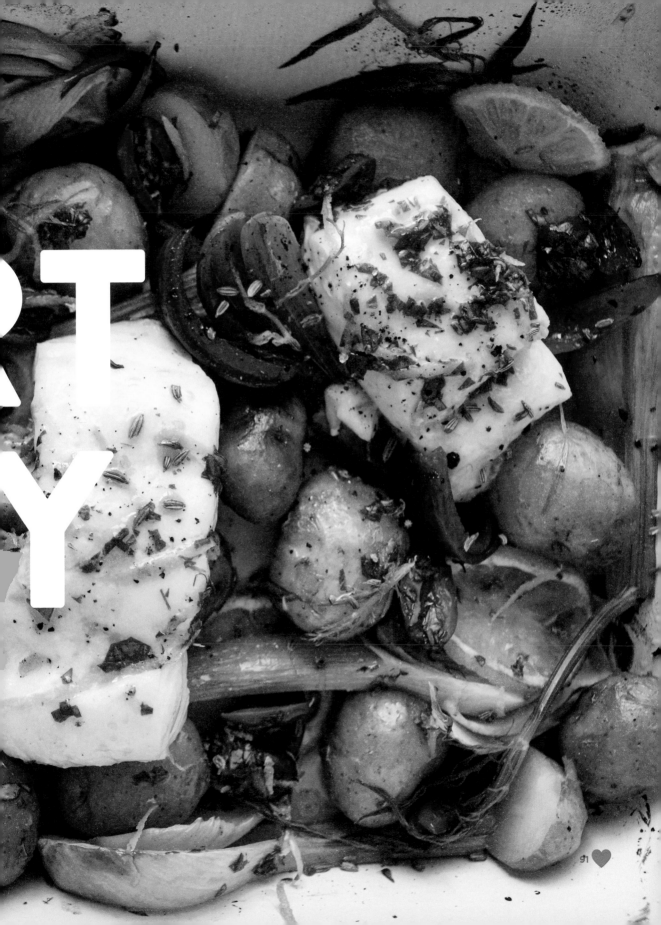

I heart family. My mother always says preparing a healthy and tasty meal for the family is one of life's greatest pleasures – and pressures. With the many demands of family life, even the most enthusiastic cook can struggle to come up with new ideas week in week out and not rely on convenience foods to serve up a meal at the end of a long day.

So, in this chapter you'll find a variety of wholesome, healthy recipes, most of which can have you calling out, *'Supper's ready!'* in an hour or less. As with all the recipes in this book, cooking from scratch is a healthy habit to get into. It can take a little longer but it's the best way to know what's in the meal that you and your family are eating.

BUTTERNUT & APPLE SOUP

SERVES 4 **PREPARE** 10 MINS **COOK** 20 MINS

1 tsp vegetable oil

1 onion, chopped

1 clove garlic, crushed

¼ tsp chilli flakes (optional)

½ tsp ground cinnamon

½ tsp ground ginger

1 butternut squash, deseeded and diced (about 1kg)

2 eating apples, cored and diced

1 litre homemade vegetable stock | page 15 | or ready-made, low-salt alternative

To serve: 4 tbsp pumpkin seeds, toasted

4 tsp low-fat natural yoghurt

 207 Kcal
869 kJ

There are some lovely flavours in this earthy, sweet and satisfying soup. Butternut squash is low in fat, but delivers on dietary fibre, making it a heart-friendly choice.

It's worth making a double batch of this one in the autumn when squash are in season – enjoy one as a family meal and freeze the rest for another day.

Heat the oil in a large saucepan and fry the onion and garlic for 3–4 minutes. Add the chilli (if using), cinnamon and ginger with the diced squash and apples and cook for 1–2 minutes.

Pour over the stock, cover and bring to the boil, then simmer for 15 minutes until tender. Purée using a hand-held blender until smooth. Season to taste with black pepper.

Serve topped with the toasted pumpkin seeds and a drizzle of yoghurt.

Note: Making soups from scratch is a great way to keep your salt intake down as you can add all sorts of other seasonings.

MAKING SOUPS CAN KEEP YOUR
SALT INTAKE DOWN AS YOU CAN
ADD YOUR OWN SEASONING

95

BEEF & LENTIL COTTAGE PIE

SERVES 4-6 **PREPARE** 30 MINS **COOK** 30-35 MINS

For the filling:

1 tbsp olive oil

1 small onion, finely chopped

2 carrots (about 200g), coarsely grated

1 celery stick, finely chopped

400g extra lean minced beef (5% fat)

200g (half a 400g can) lentils in water, drained and rinsed

50g tomato purée

500ml homemade beef stock | page 15 | or ready-made, low-salt alternative

1 tbsp Worcestershire sauce

For the topping:

550g floury potatoes, peeled and cubed

550g sweet potatoes, peeled and cubed

1 tbsp sunflower spread

2 tbsp skimmed milk

100g spinach, coarsely chopped

496 Kcal
2083 kJ

The whole family will love the flavours in this tasty, rustic pie. The lentils are a great addition as they make the meat go further while adding protein and fibre. And if you're worried about how picky eaters might react to them, don't be – the lentils are well disguised under the cover of the sauce and a golden potato topping!

Heat the oil in a large frying pan and gently fry the onion with the carrot and celery for about 5 minutes, or until softened, but not coloured. Add the mince and cook until browned. Stir in the remaining filling ingredients. Season with black pepper, then gently cook for about 20 minutes, until the liquid has reduced. Spoon into a 1.5 litre ovenproof shallow dish.

Meanwhile, preheat the oven to 190°C/gas mark 5. Place the floury potatoes in a pan and just cover with cold water and bring to the boil. Simmer for 5 minutes, add the sweet potato and return to the boil, then cook for a further 10 minutes or until both types of potatoes are tender.

Drain thoroughly, then return to the pan. Mash until smooth, before stirring in the remaining ingredients. Spoon the mash over the mince to cover. Bake for 30–35 minutes until the top is crisp and golden and the centre is piping hot. Serve with garden peas, beans or any other seasonal green vegetables.

Note: Make sure everything has cooled before putting the topping on, otherwise it will sink into the mince. Other combinations of root vegetables make good toppings, too – try swede and carrot mash for a change.

"A cottage pie is a family favourite of mine and reminds me of my childhood, but this is a healthier version! I always want something hearty, especially in the winter. Beef is obviously full of iron, and lentils are great for protein and fibre. Perfect for after a big workout!"

REBECCA ADLINGTON OBE

MUSHROOM & PARMESAN CRUSTLESS QUICHES

SERVES 6 **PREPARE** 10 MINS **COOK** 20 MINS

Sunflower oil spray

1 tsp vegetable oil

1 red onion, sliced

250g mixed mushrooms, trimmed and thickly sliced

2 large handfuls of rocket, roughly chopped (50g)

4 medium eggs

1 tbsp freshly grated Parmigiano Reggiano (about 15g)

108 Kcal
449 kJ

These little quiches are much lower in saturated fat and salt than the standard recipe, since they're packed with mushrooms and rocket instead of loads of pastry, bacon, cream and cheese.

Satisfyingly substantial, they also hold their shape well, so they're great for popping into a bag and enjoying on journeys or at the office.

Preheat the oven to 190°C/gas mark 5. Spray six holes of a muffin tray with a little oil. Heat the oil in a non-stick frying pan, add the onion and cook over a low heat for 6–7 minutes, until softened. Stir in the mushrooms, cover with a small piece of damp greaseproof paper and cook for a further 2–3 minutes, then stir in the rocket and allow to wilt slightly.

Whisk the eggs with a little black pepper until frothy. Remove the paper from the mushrooms and stir over a high heat for 1 minute to allow any moisture to evaporate.

Spoon the mushroom and onion mixture evenly between prepared muffin tin holes, then pour the eggs over. Bake in the preheated oven for 10 minutes. When nearly set, sprinkle over the cheese and return to the oven for a further 2–3 minutes, or until the quiches are set and golden in colour.

Allow to stand for 5 minutes before turning out of the tray. Serve warm with a tomato salad.

HOMEMADE BAKED BEANS

SERVES 4-6 **PREPARE** 15 MINS **COOK** 15 MINS

75g unsmoked back bacon, chopped

1 small onion, finely chopped

1 stick celery, finely chopped

1 clove garlic, crushed

2×400g cans chopped tomatoes

2 tbsp black treacle

2 tbsp tomato purée

2×400g cans pinto beans, drained and rinsed

15g fresh flat-leaf parsley, chopped

196 Kcal
826 kJ

I love these beans piled on toasted rye or sourdough, then topped with a poached egg and a pinch of chilli flakes – perfect for a really earthy breakfast or simple Sunday night supper.

Heat a large saucepan and add the bacon. Fry for 1 minute, then add the onion, celery and garlic and continue to fry for 4–5 minutes until the bacon is cooked and the onion has started to soften.

Stir in the chopped tomatoes, black treacle and tomato purée. Bring to a simmer, then stir in the beans. Continue to simmer for about 10 minutes.

Stir the chopped parsley into the beans, then serve over toast or with Tarragon Chicken Goujons | page 101 |.

Note: These would also be good topped with a piece of meaty fish like cod, monkfish or hake, plus lots of fresh herbs for extra flavour.

THE MIX OF WHOLEMEAL BREADCRUMBS
AND OATMEAL ADDS FIBRE

TARRAGON CHICKEN GOUJONS

SERVES 4 **PREPARE** 15 MINS **COOK** 35 MINS

50g wholemeal breadcrumbs

50g oatmeal

1 tbsp chopped tarragon

2 medium eggs, beaten

30–40g plain flour

350g chicken mini fillets

Vegetable oil spray

243 Kcal
1026 kJ

"Eating with my family is one of my favourite things to do. We always try to keep it healthy and balanced for the kids, and it is also important for me to get the protein and nutrients I need for training and performing on the pitch. This Tarragon Chicken recipe is a really tasty and healthy version of a classic children's dinner that can be enjoyed by the whole family."

ADAM LALLANA

Goujons are a firm teatime favourite with children and making your own means you can guarantee the goodness. Coating the goujons with a mix of wholemeal breadcrumbs and oatmeal adds fibre, while the tarragon is a lovely accompaniment to the chicken, adding flavour without salt.

Preheat the oven to 200°C/gas mark 6. Take three shallow bowls: in one of the bowls stir together the breadcrumbs, oatmeal and tarragon, then place the beaten eggs and flour in each of the remaining bowls.

Using a piece of kitchen paper, dry the chicken fillets, then quickly dip first into the flour to lightly coat, then into the beaten eggs, and finally roll in the herby breadcrumb mix. Place on a baking sheet and repeat for each piece of chicken. Generously spray the chicken with the vegetable oil and bake for 10–15 minutes, or until the chicken is thoroughly cooked and there is no pink meat.

Serve with a green salad or Homemade Baked Beans | page 99 | and a slice of lemon.

Note: If you want to vary it, make game goujons using strips of partridge or pheasant breast fillets in place of the chicken fillets. Serve with Celeriac Chips | page 140 | and Roast Beetroot | page 138 |.

PORTOBELLO MUSHROOM MARGARITA

SERVES 4 (AS A STARTER OR 2 AS A MAIN) **PREPARE** 10 MINS **COOK** 25 MINS

4 large portobello
mushrooms, peeled

250g cherry tomatoes, halved

1 tbsp olive oil

2 cloves garlic, crushed

20g black olives, sliced

80g reduced-fat mozzarella,
drained, sliced and torn

A handful of basil leaves,
roughly torn (10g)

To serve: Salad leaves (optional)

Drizzle of either balsamic glaze or
pomegranate molasses (optional)

66 Kcal
276 kJ

Every member of the family will love this quirky take on a traditional pizza. It's great for brunch, breakfast or as a substantial snack, and the portobello mushrooms make it a tasty way to up your family's veg intake.

Preheat the oven to 200°C/gas mark 6. Remove and slice the mushroom stalks and place with the tomatoes in a roasting tin with the olive oil and garlic. Season and roast for 15 minutes.

Meanwhile, place the mushrooms on a baking tray, stalk side up. When the tomato mixture is ready, spoon into the mushrooms, scatter with the sliced olives and top with the mozzarella.

Bake for 10 minutes until the cheese is golden. Season with freshly ground black pepper, then serve scattered with basil leaves and a crisp green salad, drizzled balsamic vinegar or pomegranate molasses.

HIRAL & HINA'S
STORY

When someone lives with a heart condition it affects not only them but their whole family. Hiral was just five years old when her mother Hina had a heart attack.

The mother and daughter were at home in the kitchen making desserts for Diwali when Hina felt unwell and went to lie down.

When Hina's father saw she was having trouble breathing, he called for an ambulance and Hina was immediately taken to hospital.

Not wanting Hiral to worry, the young girl's grandmother stayed at home with her and they carried on making the desserts together.

In hospital Hina had two stents fitted to open up one of her blocked coronary arteries (which supply blood to the heart muscle) and was put on medication including statins, a drug that helps reduce cholesterol levels in the blood.

Hiral was relieved to see her mother return home and make a full recovery with the support of cardiac rehabilitation – a programme of exercise and information sessions designed to help people get back on their feet after a heart attack, heart surgery or procedure.

Hina explained to her daughter what had happened, and although it was a scary experience, it also had the positive effect of bringing the family even closer together.

Although all the stories in this book are as unique as the remarkable people sharing them, I discovered they all have something special in common. The worry associated with having a heart condition is far outweighed by the love of family and friends and the support of the medical teams and charities like the BHF.

MIXED GRAIN & HALLOUMI SALAD

SERVES 4 **PREPARE** 10 MINS **COOK** 15 MINS

500ml hot homemade vegetable stock | page 15 | or ready-made, low-salt alternative

60g three-colour quinoa blend

60g bulgur wheat

1 preserved lemon

200g cherry tomatoes, halved

400g can chickpeas, drained and rinsed

A bunch of chives, chopped (about 25g)

A handful of mint leaves (about 20g)

70g rocket

Juice of ½ lemon, plus lemon wedges to serve

Olive oil spray

120g reduced-fat halloumi, sliced into 8 pieces

25g mixed seeds, toasted (optional)

275 Kcal
1156 kJ

This salad is full of wholesome ingredients and is quick to throw together. Quinoa and bulgur wheat are rich in protein and minerals, and add a subtly nutty taste to the dish. A little reduced-fat halloumi is a good source of calcium – but keep portions small as it's still high in salt and saturated fat.

Heat the stock in a pan and bring to the boil, add the quinoa and bulgur wheat and simmer gently for 10–12 minutes or until the grains are cooked and tender. Drain and tip into a serving bowl.

Dice the preserved lemon rind, discarding the flesh, and stir it into the grains along with the tomatoes, chickpeas, chives, mint and rocket with the lemon juice. Cover.

Spray a non-stick frying pan or griddle pan with a little oil and cook the cheese for 1–2 minutes on each side, until golden in colour. Serve on top of the salad with a wedge of lemon to squeeze over and a scattering of mixed seeds, if you wish.

Note: Cook the halloumi just before you serve as it goes chewy very quickly when left to cool.

BEEF & BARLEY STEW

SERVES 4 **PREPARE** 10 MINS **COOK** 2 HOURS 15 MINS

1 tsp sunflower oil

400g diced braising steak

1 onion, roughly chopped

2 sticks celery, roughly chopped

1 carrot, roughly chopped

2 tbsp tomato purée

2 cloves garlic, finely chopped

150ml red wine

500ml homemade beef stock
| page 15 | or ready-made,
low-salt alternative

400g can chopped tomatoes

3 sprigs thyme

2 bay leaves

50g pearl barley

To serve: large handful of
parsley, chopped

Steamed shredded Savoy
cabbage (optional)

280 Kcal
1176 kJ

This rustic dish has a sweet tomato sauce packed with tender beef, but it's the pearl barley that really makes it. Pearl barley is a nutritious grain with a mild, nutty flavour and it thickens the stew to create a wonderfully wholesome texture.

Heat the oil in a large casserole pan, add the beef in batches and cook until golden brown. Remove with a slotted spoon and set aside.

Add the onion, celery, carrot and a splash of water to the casserole pan and fry for a further 3–4 minutes, until softened. Add the tomato purée and garlic and fry for a further minute.

Return the beef to the casserole and pour in the wine with the stock, chopped tomatoes, thyme and bay leaves. Season generously with black pepper. Bring to the boil, cover and simmer gently for 1½ hours.

Add the pearl barley and simmer for 30 minutes until the beef and barley are both very tender. Serve scattered with parsley or with steamed shredded Savoy cabbage.

Note: If you prefer to cook this in the oven rather than on the hob, it will take about 2 hours at 170°C/gas mark 3.

"I love my food. When I'm in training, the right balance of protein and carbohydrate is important to help repair muscle, and of course it needs to taste good. The beef is the protein provider and pearl barley is a high-fibre carbohydrate – a great protein-carb combo in one pot."

ALISTAIR BROWNLEE MBE

SPRING CHICKEN & DILL BRAISE

SERVES 4 **PREPARE** 15 MINS **COOK** 25 MINS

500ml homemade chicken
stock | page 15 | or ready-made,
low-salt alternative

8 skinless, boneless chicken thighs,
cut into chunks

150g chantenay, baby carrots
or carrots, halved or cut into batons

1 small leek, thinly sliced

4 little gem lettuce hearts, halved

150g peas

75g broad beans, double podded

2 tbsp half-fat crème fraîche

Half a bunch of chopped
dill (4 tbsp)

To serve: 250g brown basmati
and wild rice

194 Kcal
814 kJ

The delicate flavours of this broth-like dish are light and clean, and it's also very easy to prepare. Using half-fat crème fraîche gives a rich flavour with less saturated fat than cream-based sauces.

Place the stock and chicken in a large saucepan and bring to the boil. Cover and simmer for 10 minutes, then add the carrots and leek. Simmer for a further 10 minutes until the vegetables are almost cooked through.

Add the lettuce, peas and beans. Cover and cook for a further 4–5 minutes until the veg are tender and chicken is cooked through with no pink meat. Remove from the heat, then stir through the crème fraîche and dill. Ladle into large soup bowls and serve with rice on the side.

CAPONATA PANZANELLA

SERVES 4 **PREPARE** 20 MINS **COOK** 40–45 MINS

200g wholewheat
or rye bread, torn

400g shallots, peeled

2 aubergines, cubed
(about 500g)

1 garlic bulb, separated
into unpeeled cloves

400g cherry tomatoes on the vine
(ideally a mix of red and yellow)

2 tsp olive oil

2 tsp balsamic vinegar

25g toasted pine nuts

50g pitted green olives,
drained and chopped

A bunch of basil leaves, roughly
torn (25g)

A bunch of flat-leaf parsley (20g)

 294 Kcal
1233 kJ

Here's a lovely side dish or starter that will add a bit of Italian flavour to any summer buffet. It's rustic and flavoursome, great with grilled, roasted or barbecued meat.

Unlike other salads with delicate leaves, this improves when left to stand, so make it up to an hour before you plan to eat. The croutons can be prepared the morning before, so it's a great choice if you've got people coming over or need to prepare in advance of a busy day ahead.

Preheat the oven to 200°C/gas mark 6. Arrange the bread in a single layer on a baking tray and bake for 10 minutes until golden. Remove from the oven and set aside.

Meanwhile, place the whole shallots, aubergine, garlic cloves and cherry tomatoes in a roasting tin and mix in the oil. Roast for 35–40 minutes or until all the vegetables are tender and lightly browned. Remove from the oven and tip into a large serving bowl with the toasted bread.

Stir in the balsamic vinegar, toasted pine nuts, olives, basil leaves and parsley. Serve while still warm or at room temperature if you prefer.

RAINBOW PEPPER STEAK FAJITAS

SERVES 4 **PREPARE** 10 MINS **COOK** 5 MINS

400g fillet or sirloin steak

1 tsp sunflower oil

2 tsp baharat spice mix

1 yellow pepper, deseeded
and cut into strips

2 red peppers, deseeded
and cut into strips

1 red onion, thinly sliced

A handful of coriander leaves (10g)

To serve: 4 soft wholemeal
tortilla wraps

4 tbsp reduced-fat guacamole

Low-fat natural yoghurt

1 little gem lettuce, shredded

420 Kcal
1764 kJ

The baharat spice in these spicy and colourful steak fajitas has
a delicious taste without the added salt that's in many pre-mixed
spice blends. Choose a lean cut of meat for lower saturated fat
and you have the perfect fast, healthy meal.

Remove and discard any of the visible fat from the steak and then
cut into thin strips. Place the beef in a bowl with the oil and spice
mix and turn to coat in the spice.

Heat a large, non-stick frying pan. When hot add the beef, peppers
and onions and stir-fry over a high heat for 7–8 minutes, until
lightly browned and the peppers and onions have softened. Stir
in the coriander.

Serve the beef and pepper mix wrapped in warm wholemeal tortillas
with a little guacamole, low-fat yoghurt and shredded lettuce.

Note: As an alternative to tortillas, wrap the filling in a large iceberg
lettuce leaf.

CHICKEN WITH RED CABBAGE & APPLE

SERVES 4 **PREPARE** 15 MINS **COOK** 20-25 MINS

500g boneless, skinless
chicken breast

1 tsp sweet smoked paprika

2 tsp olive oil

1 red onion, finely sliced

400g red cabbage,
finely shredded

½–1 tsp dried crushed chillies

1 apple, quartered, cored and cut
into matchsticks (about 200g)

75g half-fat crème fraîche

267 Kcal
1116 kJ

This is a cosy and warming dish that makes a nice alternative to braised red cabbage on a chilly autumn or winter evening. Being straightforward to put together, it's the perfect choice for a weeknight meal.

Dust the chicken breasts with the paprika. Heat a non-stick frying pan with 1 tsp of the oil, add the chicken and cook for about 10–12 minutes, turning occasionally, or until the chicken is thoroughly cooked and there is no pink meat.

Meanwhile, heat the remaining oil in a saucepan and fry the onion for about 5 minutes until it starts to brown. Add the cabbage and crushed chillies, cover and cook for a further 5 minutes, stirring occasionally.

Add the apple and cook gently, covered, for about 10 minutes until the vegetables have softened but still retain a little bite.

Serve the cabbage spooned onto warmed serving plates and top with a chicken breast. Stir the crème fraîche and 1 tbsp of water into the pan juices and pour over the chicken.

Serve with cooked green beans or broccoli.

CHICKEN & LEEK CASSEROLE

SERVES 4 **PREPARE** 15 MINS **COOK** 30 MINS

1 tsp olive oil

500g boneless, skinless
chicken breast

400g leeks, trimmed
and thinly sliced

400g can haricot beans,
drained and rinsed

4 sprigs fresh thyme

1 fresh bay leaf

300ml homemade chicken
stock | page 15 | or ready-made,
low-salt alternative

A bunch of fresh flat-leaf parsley,
coarsely chopped (20g)

234 Kcal
989 kJ

This recipe is a great wholesome midweek supper to have in your repertoire. Adding extra vegetables and beans to a casserole helps you towards your five a day while also making the meat go further.

Heat the oil in a non-stick sauté pan and cook the chicken over a high heat until browned on both sides. Remove from the pan, drain on kitchen paper and keep warm.

Add the leeks to the pan and cook over a low heat for 3–4 minutes until softened but not browned. Add the beans, thyme, bay leaf and stock, cover and simmer for a further 4 minutes.

Arrange the chicken on top of the beans, cover the pan and cook over a low heat for 15–20 minutes until the chicken is cooked through. Scatter with flat-leaf parsley and serve with pearl barley, steamed broccoli florets and some wilted chard or asparagus.

Note: You can also serve with some healthier garlic bread, made by rubbing a halved garlic clove over slices of toasted wholegrain baguette and drizzling over a little olive oil.

CHIPOTLE VEGGIE BEAN BURGER

SERVES 4 **PREPARE** 30 MINS PLUS COOLING **COOK** 25-30 MINS

For the burger:

175g butternut squash, diced

175g sweet potato, diced

200g potato, peeled and diced

400g can red kidney beans, drained and rinsed

1 tbsp chipotle paste (about 20g)

2 spring onions, thinly sliced

Half a bunch of fresh coriander, chopped

75g frozen sweetcorn, thawed and patted dry with a clean tea towel

40g fresh wholemeal breadcrumbs

3-4 sprays sunflower oil spray

For the salsa:

2 tomatoes, chopped

A handful of coriander leaves, chopped (10g)

Half a small red onion, finely diced (30g)

Lime juice, to taste

For the chipotle mayonnaise:

2 tbsp reduced-fat mayonnaise

¼ – ½ tsp chipotle paste

266 Kcal
1117 kJ

If you're not convinced that a veggie dish can be tasty and satisfying, just try this one. Trust me, it'll be a big hit! These burgers make a lovely lunch or barbecue dish and you can make them in advance. They count towards your five a day and are a source of fibre.

Preheat the oven to 200°C/gas mark 6, and line a baking tray with baking parchment. Arrange the butternut squash and sweet potato in a single layer and roast for 20 minutes or until tender and starting to colour. Remove from the oven and leave on one side to cool.

Place the potatoes in a pan of water, bring to the boil and simmer for 5-10 minutes until the potatoes are tender, drain thoroughly and allow to cool and dry in a sieve.

In a bowl, mix together the cooled potatoes and beans, and mash them together using a potato masher. Stir in the chipotle paste and add the spring onions, coriander leaves, sweetcorn, cooked butternut and sweet potato mix – pressing down with a spoon to slightly crush. Season with black pepper, and mix well to combine and evenly distribute the vegetables.

With damp hands, divide the mixture into 4 and shape into burgers. Lightly press the breadcrumbs over the surface of each of the burgers, and transfer onto the prepared baking tray. Give each burger a spray of the sunflower oil. Bake in the preheated oven for 25-30 minutes, until the burgers are piping hot and golden.

Meanwhile, mix the salsa ingredients together and then, in a separate bowl, mix together the ingredients for the chipotle mayonnaise. Serve the burgers topped with the chipotle mayonnaise, a generous portion of the tomato salsa on the side and some Sweet Potato Wedges | page 140 |.

MADE FROM THE HEART

Cooking from scratch not only gives you a sense of satisfaction but will also help you keep your heart healthy. Knowing what's in your meals, rather than buying ready-made or processed foods that can be high in salt and saturated fat, will give you more control over your diet.

When I met Gabriela I couldn't believe this cheerful, fun-loving little girl was the heroine of such a heart-breaking story.

Shortly after Gabriela's birth, her mother Cherilyn felt something was wrong and took her to the doctor. At only four weeks old, a heart murmur was detected. It was every parent's nightmare and the beginning of a long and challenging journey for the Atkins family.

Further tests discovered several heart problems and during the first year of her life Gabriela underwent a series of procedures to manage her condition.

Throughout this difficult period Cherilyn and her husband Rudi relied heavily on the support of their families and a dedicated team of doctors and nurses.

Gabriela spent her first Christmas in hospital and a few months later underwent a nine-hour heart operation. The surgery was a success but she wasn't out of the woods yet, and further operations followed.

Today Gabriela's beautiful smile belies the traumatic start to her life.

Full of beans, she enjoys dancing, gymnastics and playing with her younger sister Bella, and has already decided what she wants to be when she grows up. A nurse.

LEMON, RED ONION & FENNEL COD TRAYBAKE

SERVES 4 **PREPARE** 10 MINS **COOK** 40 MINS

1 lemon

400g new potatoes

4 small fennel bulbs, trimmed, cored and thickly sliced (fronds reserved)

1 red onion, sliced (about 180g)

2 tbsp olive oil

4 skinless and boneless cod fillets (each about 125g)

1 tsp fennel seeds, crushed

2 tbsp white wine vinegar

A handful of basil leaves, chopped (10g)

25g pitted black olives, halved

311 Kcal
1302 kJ

This dish doesn't just look pretty, it's also full of fantastic flavours. The herbs and spices add plenty of interest and the olives are carefully balanced to give the dish extra depth without adding too much salt. Although light to eat, it's still satisfyingly filling as the cod is a great source of protein.

Preheat the oven to 200°C/gas mark 6. Finely grate the zest of 1 lemon, then thinly slice it and set aside. Toss the potatoes and fennel in a large baking tray with the onion and lemon slices and 1 tbsp oil. Spread in a single layer and bake for 25–30 minutes, or until the potatoes are cooked.

Place the cod on top, sprinkle with the crushed fennel seeds and season with black pepper. Bake for another 10–12 minutes, or until the fish is just cooked through.

Meanwhile, make the dressing: whisk together the vinegar with the remaining oil, then add the basil, olives and lemon zest, season and mix together. Pour over the fish, scatter with any reserved fennel fronds and serve.

HALIBUT WITH ROAST TOMATO & HERB DRESSING

SERVES 4 **PREPARE** 10 MINS PLUS SOAKING **COOK** 30 MINS

4 dry-packed sun-dried tomatoes

1 small red onion, finely sliced

2 tsp red wine vinegar

2½ tbsp olive oil

4×180g halibut steaks

200g cherry tomatoes, quartered

25g flat-leaf parsley, chopped

25g basil, chopped

244 Kcal
1022 kJ

Halibut is a delicious white fish with large flakes and a firm but tender texture. It's best cooked on the bone to help seal in the flavoursome juices. The tangy tomato dressing sets it off perfectly, while home-pickled onions add a bit of texture.

This would be lovely served with a helping of puy lentils and the Chargrilled Asparagus and Broccoli with Feta | page 202 |.

In a small bowl, cover the sun-dried tomatoes with boiling water and leave to soak for 20 minutes, then drain and chop.

Preheat the oven to 200°C/gas mark 6. Place the sliced onion in the vinegar and leave to infuse.

Place the halibut steaks on a baking sheet lined with baking parchment. Brush the fish with half a tablespoon of the olive oil and roast in the oven for 10–15 minutes, until the fish is starting to flake and is just cooked.

In a small saucepan, gently warm the remaining oil, then add the sun-dried tomatoes and cherry tomatoes until the cherry tomatoes start to soften. This should take about 5 minutes.

Add the infused onion and vinegar and continue to cook for a further 2 minutes. Remove from the heat and stir in the herbs. Serve the sauce warm, and spooned over the roasted fish.

GINGER CHICKEN STIR-FRY

SERVES 4 **PREPARE** 10 MINS **COOK** 10 MINS

400g chicken breast mini fillets, sliced in half lengthways

4 cm piece root ginger, peeled and grated

1 clove garlic, crushed

3 tbsp sweet chilli sauce

1 tsp vegetable oil

200g trimmed fine green beans, cut in half

200g courgette, cut into 3 cm long strips

½ Chinese leaf cabbage, or 200g pak choi, thickly sliced

1 bunch spring onions, thickly sliced

A handful of coriander leaves

180 Kcal
762 kJ

Here's a quick and easy dish with some lovely flavours – perfect for a midweek supper. Making your own stir-fry helps keep your salt intake down and is a great way to pack loads of vegetables into your meal.

Mix together the chicken, ginger, garlic and 1 tbsp of the chilli sauce, and leave for 10 minutes.

Heat the oil in a wok and, when hot, add the chicken and stir-fry for 3–4 minutes. Stir in the beans, courgette and cabbage and cook for a further 4–5 minutes.

Stir in the spring onions and remaining sweet chilli sauce and cook for a few seconds more. Scatter over the coriander leaves and serve with steamed wholegrain rice, buckwheat soba or rice noodles.

ROAST TOMATO & BASIL SPELT RISOTTO

SERVES 4 **PREPARE** 10 MINS **COOK** 50 MINS

400g tomatoes, quartered

500g cherry tomatoes

Extra virgin olive oil spray

750ml–1 litre homemade vegetable stock | page 15 | or ready-made, low-salt alternative

Large pinch of saffron threads

1 small leek, finely sliced

4 cloves garlic, crushed

200g quick-cook farro or pearled spelt, rinsed

Handful basil leaves, roughly torn

100g baby spinach leaves

To serve: 4 tbsp pumpkin seeds, toasted

Fresh Grana Padano or Parmigiano Reggiano (optional)

Watercress salad (optional)

353 Kcal
1483 kJ

This wholesome risotto is lovely for lunch and also makes a delicious side dish for griddled meat or fish. It uses pearled spelt instead of the usual risotto rice, giving it a nuttiness that goes really well with the sweet tomatoes.

Preheat the oven to 200°C/gas mark 6. Place both varieties of tomato in a single layer in a large roasting tin. Spray lightly with olive oil and roast for about 20 minutes, until tender but holding their shape.

Meanwhile, place the stock in a pan and bring to the boil, add the saffron threads and leave to infuse.

Heat a large frying pan, sprayed with a little of the oil, add the leek and gently cook for 3–4 minutes, or until softened. Then add the garlic and cook for a minute. Finally, stir in the spelt with the basil and half of the tomatoes.

Pour in a third of the hot stock and leave at a gentle simmer, stirring occasionally. Gradually add the remaining two-thirds of the stock until it has all been absorbed.

When the spelt is tender and the stock absorbed, gently stir in the spinach with the remaining tomatoes.

Serve with Parmesan shavings (if using), toasted pumpkin seeds and a watercress salad.

MEATBALLS WITH TABBOULEH

SERVES 4 **PREPARE** 15 MINS **COOK** 15–20 MINS

For the meatballs:

3 tsp olive oil

1 clove garlic, crushed

1 small onion, very finely chopped (120g)

500g turkey mince

2 tsp ras el hanout spice mix

A bunch of fresh parsley, chopped (25g)

For the tabbouleh:

250g pouch mixed cooked grains such as quinoa, chickpeas, bulgur wheat & rice (or barley, wheat berries, spelt & rice)

80g spinach, washed

2 bunches of flat-leaf parsley, stalks removed (50g)

25g mint, stalks removed

200g pomegranate seeds

1 bunch spring onions, washed and thinly sliced

Coarsely grated zest and juice of 1 lemon

2 tbsp pomegranate molasses

To serve: Roasted Cucumber Tzatziki | page 67 | and Homemade Houmous | page 73 |

362 Kcal
1528 kJ

Give the classic Middle-Eastern tabbouleh a makeover with this super-speedy yet healthy midweek meal. If you love the original, I think you're in for a treat.

For the meatballs, preheat the oven to 180°C/gas mark 4. In a non-stick frying pan, heat up 1 tsp of olive oil, add the garlic and chopped onion and fry gently for 2–3 minutes, or until the onions have softened. Remove from the heat and allow to cool slightly.

Tip the cooked onion mixture into a bowl with the minced turkey and remaining meatball ingredients. Mix together until it is thoroughly and evenly mixed. Then divide and roll this mixture into 20 evenly sized balls.

Heat 2 tsp olive oil in a frying pan and sear the meatballs for about 5 minutes until golden all over. Transfer onto a baking tray lined with baking parchment. Cook in the oven for 10 minutes, or until the meatballs are cooked through and there is no pink meat.

While the meatballs are cooking, make the tabbouleh. Cook the mixed grains according to the instructions on the pack, tip into a mixing bowl and allow to cool. Meanwhile, roughly chop the spinach and herbs, and add to the bowl with the pomegranate seeds, spring onions and lemon zest. Mix thoroughly so everything is evenly distributed, then whisk together the pomegranate molasses and lemon juice and pour over the salad.

Serve the salad with the meatballs and a spoonful of Roasted Cucumber Tzatziki and Homemade Houmous.

TURKEY CHILLI RAGU

SERVES 4 **PREPARE** 10 MINS **COOK** 40 MINS

Olive oil spray

1 onion, chopped

1 large carrot, diced

1 celery stick, diced

2 cloves garlic, chopped

1 red chilli, deseeded
and chopped

2 tsp thyme leaves,
stalks discarded

500g turkey mince

2×400g cans chopped
tomatoes

400g can kidney beans,
drained and rinsed

6 dry-packed sundried
tomatoes, chopped

1 tsp Worcestershire sauce

300g wholewheat fusilli

To serve: Freshly grated
Parmigiano Reggiano

466 Kcal
1963 kJ

Give your traditional chilli con carne a healthy twist by using turkey mince. It's not only high in protein, it's also much lower in fat than minced pork and beef.

Spray a large saucepan with oil and cook the onion, carrot, celery and garlic for 5 minutes. Add the chilli, thyme and turkey and cook for a further 5 minutes, stirring frequently, until the vegetables are softening but not coloured.

Add the tomatoes, beans, sundried tomatoes, Worcestershire sauce and a splash of water. Bring to the boil, cover and simmer for 30 minutes (or a little longer if you have time) until thickened into a rich red sauce.

Meanwhile, cook the pasta in a large pan of boiling water for 9 minutes or until al dente. Drain well, toss with the turkey ragu and serve with a small sprinkling of Parmigiano Reggiano.

Note: As an alternative to fusilli, you can try serving with wholewheat spaghetti or courgetti.

You can also serve the turkey ragu with brown rice, more like a chilli con carne. Top it with a spoonful of low-fat Greek yoghurt, some chopped avocado and a scattering of chopped fresh chilli to taste.

DRESSED CAULIFLOWER SALAD

SERVES 4 (AS A SIDE DISH) **PREPARE** 15 MINS **COOK** 35 MINS

1 large cauliflower (about 550g)

4 tbsp extra virgin olive oil

1 clove garlic, peeled and sliced

Juice of 1 lemon

2 tbsp capers, rinsed and drained (about 25g)

1 tbsp pine nuts, lightly toasted

A handful of flat-leaf parsley, finely chopped (10g)

1 unwaxed lemon, halved

To serve: Low-fat natural yoghurt

189 Kcal
783 kJ

Cauliflower is one of my favourite vegetables – it's filling and surprisingly adaptable. Roasting the cauliflower in this salad gives it a wonderful flavour and, if you have time, you can also grill it for a charred effect around the edges.

Preheat the oven to 200°C/gas mark 6. Remove the leaves from the cauliflower and trim any excess stalk at the base. Using a large knife, cut the cauliflower into florets, toss in a tablespoon of the olive oil and then arrange in a single layer in a roasting tin.

Cover with foil and roast in the oven for 30–35 minutes until tender, removing the foil halfway through.

Meanwhile, warm the remaining olive oil in a small pan with the garlic slices, take off the heat and leave to infuse for 5 minutes. Remove the garlic from the olive oil and discard, then whisk in the lemon juice. Stir in the capers, pine nuts and parsley.

Remove the cauliflower from the oven and transfer to a serving dish. Drizzle the dressing over, season, then squeeze over extra lemon juice to taste, and serve with a spoonful of yoghurt.

Note: Cooked cauliflower discolours within a few hours – so this dish is best eaten when freshly cooked.

ROAST BEETROOT

SERVES 4 **PREPARE** 5 MINS **COOK** 40–45 MINS

500g raw beetroot

4 cloves unpeeled garlic

A handful of fresh thyme (10g)

2 tbsp balsamic vinegar

1 tbsp olive oil

Black pepper

White balsamic vinegar,
to taste

Lemon thyme, to taste

 87 Kcal
364 kJ

Beetroot is a fantastically versatile vegetable. When it's in season I try to add some to my salads as often as possible, not just for the nutritional value, but also for its wonderful jewel-like colour.

Try the golden variety as well – cooking and preparing instructions are the same.

Preheat the oven to 200°C/gas mark 6. Scrub the beetroot, trim and cut each into 4–6 wedges. Place in the centre of a large piece of foil.

Place the garlic cloves on top of the beetroot and scatter with the sprigs of thyme. Season with black pepper and fold the edges of the foil together to make a parcel that is sealed on three sides, leaving one flap open.

Add the balsamic and olive oil to the beetroot and seal the foil parcel completely, transfer onto a baking sheet and bake in the oven for 40–45 minutes, or until the beetroot is tender.

Serve as a vegetable side seasoned with plenty of black pepper, a drizzle of white balsamic and scattered with lemon thyme.

Note: To make this into a main meal for lunch, toss the warm beetroot wedges with 100g rocket leaves and scatter over 50g crumbled reduced-fat feta.

For a delicious dressing, drizzle with the beetroot juices and a little extra white balsamic.

SWEET POTATO WEDGES

SERVES 2 **PREPARE** 5 MINS **COOK** 30 MINS

2 sweet potatoes, cut into wedges (about 500g)

1 tbsp olive oil

½ tsp sweet smoked paprika

 285 Kcal
1191 kJ

Sweet potatoes make a nutritious alternative to the standard white potatoes and also count towards your five a day. I like my wedges almost blackened at the edges to make them nice and crispy. There's almost no dish that can't be improved by a bowl of these on the side!

Preheat the oven to 220°C/gas mark 7. On a large baking tray, toss the sweet potatoes with the olive oil and paprika and season. Spread in an even layer and roast for 30 minutes, turning halfway through, until crisp.

Note: Sprinkle with dried chilli flakes for an extra hot kick.

CELERIAC CHIPS

SERVES 4 **PREPARE** 5 MINS **COOK** 40 MINS

1 medium celeriac (about 700g)

1–2 tbsp olive oil

 142 Kcal
594 kJ

Celeriac is an underrated joy. It keeps well so makes a good standby ingredient to have around the kitchen. These chips are great with Saffron Yoghurt Aioli | page 226 | or as a side dish to go with a piece of griddled fish or meat.

Preheat the oven to 200°C/gas mark 6. Using a sharp knife, peel the celeriac then cut into 2 cm thick slices, and then into thick chips.

Place the celeriac in a pan of boiling water and boil for 1–2 minutes, then drain thoroughly, toss with the olive oil and arrange in a single layer on a baking sheet. Bake in the oven for 35–40 minutes, until tender and golden in colour.

Note: Sprinkle with hot smoked paprika for some added spice and flavour.

ROAST BEETROOT
(PAGE 138)

BANANA, BLUEBERRY & OAT MUFFINS

MAKES 18 (1 PER SERVING) **PREPARE** 15 MINS **COOK** 20-25 MINS

180g plain flour

180g wholemeal plain flour

2 tsp baking powder

1 tsp bicarbonate of soda

100g golden caster sugar

250g blueberries

100g rolled oats

3 medium eggs, lightly beaten

120ml vegetable oil

100g clear honey

3-4 large ripe bananas,
mashed (about 480g)

229 Kcal
961 kJ

These are indulgent treats for all the family. Grown-ups can enjoy them without the guilt factor of the full-fat ones, and the kids will love them too – especially with the juiciness of the blueberries and the sweetness of the bananas.

There are some smart health tricks in this recipe: mixing standard flour with wholemeal means you add extra fibre without anyone noticing, and using oil rather than butter helps to keep the saturated fat down.

Preheat the oven to 190°C/gas mark 5. Meanwhile, line a muffin tin with 18 large muffin papers and set aside.

In a large bowl, combine the flours, baking powder and bicarbonate of soda, then stir in the sugar, blueberries and oats. In a separate bowl, mix the eggs, oil, honey and bananas.

Tip the wet ingredients into the dry. Mix until combined, but do not overwork. If the mix is a little stiff, add 1 tbsp milk.

Spoon the mixture into the muffin papers. Bake for 20–25 minutes or until the muffins are well risen and coloured golden brown. To test if they are cooked in the middle, insert the point of a knife or a skewer: if it comes out clean, they are ready. If the muffins are still sticky in the middle, bake them for a few more minutes.

Eat these on the day you bake them.

OATMEAL TEA LOAF

MAKES 12 SLICES (1 PER SERVING)   **PREPARE** 20 MINS PLUS SOAKING   **COOK** 60 MINS

2 tea bags

75g soft apricots, roughly chopped

75g soft prunes, roughly chopped

100g raisins

50g dates, roughly chopped

225g light brown muscovado sugar

2 medium eggs, beaten

75g oatmeal

150g wholemeal plain flour

2 tsp baking powder

1 tsp ground cinnamon

 213 Kcal
902 kJ

This loaf is really moreish: dense, fruity and moist, with great flavours and packed with dried fruits for sustained energy. Make it to enjoy alongside cups of tea over a weekend, or wrap it up to take on a picnic.

Place the tea bags in a measuring jug, pour over 300ml boiling water and allow to infuse for 4–5 minutes.

Place the dried fruit and sugar into a large bowl and strain the hot tea over, then discard the bags. Stir well, cover with cling film and leave to soak for 4–5 hours or overnight.

Preheat the oven to 180°C/gas mark 4. Grease and line a 900g loaf tin. Stir the eggs into the fruit mixture. In a separate bowl, mix together the oatmeal and flour with the baking powder and cinnamon and then stir in the fruit mixture until thoroughly combined.

Pour the mixture into the prepared tin and bake for 1 hour, or until a skewer, inserted into the middle, comes out clean. Cover the top with foil if the loaf becomes too brown while cooking.

Allow to cool in the tin for 10 minutes before transferring to a cooling rack. Serve cold, cut into slices.

SPICED BLACK FOREST CRUMBLE

SERVES 4-6 **PREPARE** 15 MINS **COOK** 40 MINS

450g frozen Black Forest
fruits, defrosted

1 tsp clear honey or agave syrup

85g wholemeal flour

55g medium oatmeal

50g low-fat spread

70g light soft brown sugar

¼ – ½ tsp ground cinnamon

 313 Kcal
1314 kJ

Incredibly comforting, but healthier than traditional crumble. Adding wholegrain oats to the topping makes this higher in fibre.

Serve hot or cold with a dollop of thick, low-fat yoghurt or a little frozen yoghurt on the side and chopped mint on top.

Preheat the oven to 190°C/gas mark 5. Tip the fruit with any juices into a 1 litre baking dish or individual ovenproof pudding bowls. Drizzle honey over the fruit.

Put the flour and oatmeal in a bowl and stir to mix. Lightly rub in the low-fat spread with your fingers until the mixture resembles breadcrumbs. Stir in the sugar and cinnamon.

Spoon this mixture evenly over the fruit and bake for 40 minutes until golden brown. Serve warm.

Note: Add some extra crunch to the crumble topping with a handful of chopped nuts, such as walnuts or almonds.

STEAMED DATE PUDDINGS

SERVES 6 **PREPARE** 15 MINS **COOK** 60 MINS

175g soft-pitted dates

1 tsp vanilla extract

100ml date syrup or maple syrup

2 large eggs, separated

80g self-raising flour

75g sultanas

To serve: fat-free yoghurt

244 Kcal
1032 kJ

"I have a sweet tooth and love my puddings but this is a healthier option. With all the training I do I have no trouble burning it off."

JONNY BROWNLEE

This is an equally lovely but healthier version of the classic sticky toffee pudding. Serve it with a spoonful of low-fat Greek yoghurt and a drizzle of date syrup.

Preheat the oven to 190°C/gas mark 5. Line the base of 6×150ml non-stick dariole moulds or ovenproof pudding bowls with a disc of baking parchment.

Place the dates in a small pan with the vanilla extract and 150ml cold water. Bring to the boil, cover, then simmer gently for 5 minutes.

Use a hand-held blender to process the cooled date mixture until smooth. Pour into a bowl, then stir in the syrup, egg yolks, flour and sultanas.

Whisk the egg whites until stiff peaks form, then gently fold into the date mixture. Spoon the sponge mixture into the prepared tins and top with a circle of baking parchment. Cover each mould firmly with a square of pleated foil.

Place the puddings in a roasting tin and pour in boiling water to reach halfway up the sides of the moulds. Bake for 45–55 minutes, topping up with boiling water if necessary, until the puddings are risen and firm.

Remove the foil and greaseproof paper, then turn the puddings out onto small plates. Serve hot with a little fat-free yoghurt on the side.

ACTIVE LIFE. HAPPY HEART.

It's not just a balanced diet that is important for good heart health. Being physically active and maintaining a healthy weight will also reduce your risk of cardiovascular disease, helping you feel more energetic in your daily life.

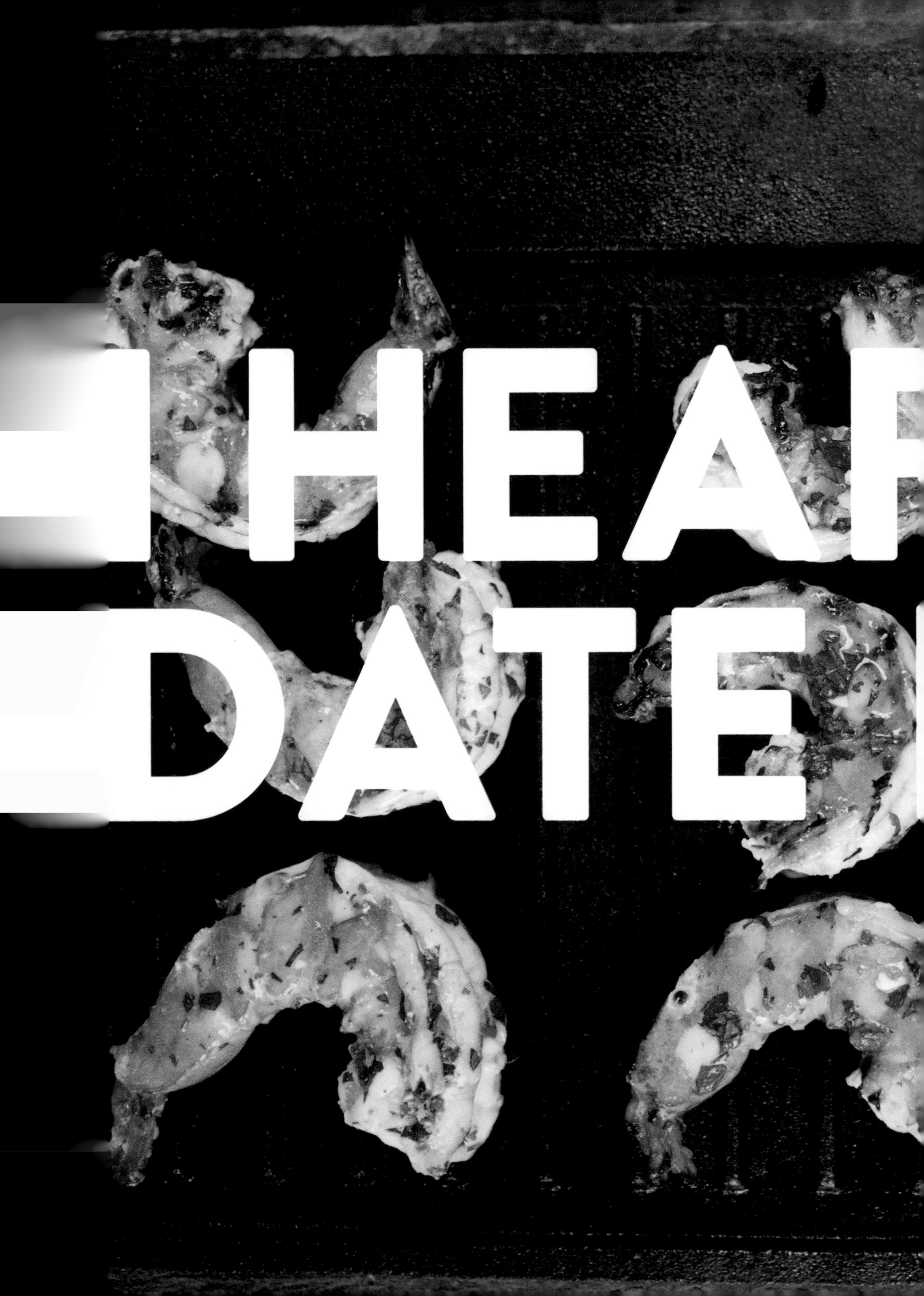
HEA
DATE

I heart date night. They say the way to a man's heart is through his stomach.

But it's not just the guys. I can think of plenty of female friends who'd happily be wooed by a lovingly made meal.

In this chapter there are plenty of delicious and healthy ideas to inspire you. So whether it's a birthday, an anniversary, or just a Monday night, treat that special someone in your life to a meal both their stomach and their heart will love.

PAN-FRIED SCALLOPS & PUY LENTIL SALAD

SERVES 2 AS A LUNCH (OR 4 AS A STARTER) **PREPARE** 10 MINS PLUS COOLING **COOK** 25 MINS

275g baby plum tomatoes, halved

125g puy lentils, rinsed

400ml homemade vegetable stock | page 15 | or ready-made, low-salt alternative

1 tbsp olive oil

6–8 large scallops, without roe

1 clove garlic, crushed

1 bunch spring onions, trimmed and sliced

1 tbsp sherry vinegar

20g wild rocket

289 Kcal
1212 kJ

"It's important that the food I choose is delicious as well as being healthy and digestible, allowing me to train easily around mealtimes. This dish brings these factors together perfectly, making it good for a light dinner or a lunch pre/post training."

ROGER FEDERER

Scallops are naturally sweet, tender and delicate in flavour while also being low in fat, but don't compromise on quality – get them as fresh as possible!

Here they're served with protein-rich puy lentils for a beautifully balanced starter or lunch with someone you want to impress.

Preheat the oven to 180°C/gas mark 4. Place the halved baby tomatoes on a baking tray and cook in the preheated oven for about 15 minutes or until softened. Remove from the oven and allow to cool slightly.

Meanwhile, place the lentils in a pan with the stock and bring to the boil, then simmer for 20 minutes or until the lentils are just tender. Strain and set aside.

Gently heat the oil in a sauté pan or deep frying pan, add the scallops and sear for about 1 minute on each side, transfer to a warm plate and cover. Return the pan to the heat, add the garlic and cook for 30 seconds to a minute before adding the spring onions, and continue to cook for 1–2 minutes or until they are beginning to soften. Then stir in the puy lentils and pan-fry for 2–3 minutes, until the lentils have heated through. Remove from the heat and set aside.

Add the softened oven-roasted tomatoes to the pan with the sherry vinegar and mix to evenly distribute, fold through the rocket and serve immediately, topped with the pan-fried scallops.

Note: Try seasoning the raw scallops with a little smoked paprika before cooking. This will add extra flavour without the need for salt.

CHINESE SALMON PARCELS

SERVES 2 **PREPARE** 10 MINS **COOK** 15-20 MINS

½ tsp rapeseed oil

2 salmon fillets, skinned (each about 140g)

1 cm piece fresh root ginger, peeled and shredded

150g pak choi, sliced

50g carrots, peeled and thinly sliced

75g chestnut mushrooms, sliced

1 tbsp low-salt soy sauce

1-2 tbsp sweet chilli dipping sauce (approx. 50g)

1 tbsp Chinese rice wine or mirin

To serve: jasmine rice, steamed or cooked rice noodles

363 Kcal
1512 kJ

I love the fresh and clean flavours in this dish, particularly the ginger. Baking in parchment paper is an easy and healthy cooking method that really helps to lock in the flavours of your ingredients. It works a treat here with the salmon – a good source of high-quality protein and omega-3 fatty acids.

Preheat the oven to 200°C/gas mark 6. Brush two large squares of baking parchment with some of the oil and place a salmon fillet in the middle of each one.

Toss together the ginger, pak choi, carrots and mushrooms. Arrange over the salmon, drizzle over the soy, chilli dipping sauce and Chinese rice wine or mirin, then fold in the baking parchment to make loose parcels.

Place on a baking sheet and bake for about 15 minutes until the salmon is just cooked and the vegetables have softened. Open the parcels and serve in bowls with jasmine rice or rice noodles.

ASIAN TUNA WITH AVOCADO SALSA

SERVES 2 **PREPARE** 5 MINS PLUS MARINATING **COOK** 8 MINS

2 fresh tuna steaks, 1.5 cm–2 cm thick (each about 240g)

For the marinade:
A handful of coriander leaves, chopped (10g)

1 red chilli, deseeded and finely sliced

1 shallot, finely sliced

Grated zest and juice of 1 lime

1 clove garlic, crushed

1 lemongrass stalk, bruised and finely chopped

1 tbsp kecap manis (Indonesian-style sweet soy sauce)

1 tbsp olive oil

For the salsa:
½ ripe avocado, stoned, peeled and diced

4 spring onions, thinly sliced

Grated zest and juice of ½ lime

2–3 red and yellow cherry tomatoes, deseeded and chopped

10g fresh coriander, roughly chopped

To serve: 1 tsp black and white sesame seeds, toasted (optional)

½ lime, cut into wedges (optional)

409 Kcal
1710 kJ

This is a brilliantly zingy and refreshing dish rich in omega-3 as it uses fresh tuna. Try to find large tuna steaks with deep purple flesh. Just sear the outside and then use a steak knife to cut into the fish, revealing the rich colour inside.

In a small bowl, mix the marinade ingredients. Season with freshly ground black pepper. Using your fingers, rub this mixture over the tuna steaks. Place in a non-metallic shallow dish and leave to marinate for 15–20 minutes.

For the salsa, combine all the ingredients in a small bowl and set aside.

Preheat an oiled griddle pan (or barbecue) to a medium-high heat. Cook the tuna steaks for 3–4 minutes on each side, until they are cooked to your liking. Garnish with coriander leaves and scatter with the toasted sesame seeds, then serve with lime wedges and a spoonful of the avocado salsa.

Note: This is also delicious served with fresh cucumber noodles and wasabi mash or quinoa.

STEAK WITH SWEET POTATO BRAVAS & WATERCRESS

SERVES 2 **PREPARE** 15 MINS **COOK** 25 MINS

300g sweet potatoes,
peeled and cut into wedges

4 tsp olive oil

½ tsp sweet smoked paprika

1 clove garlic

Pinch of chilli flakes

227g can chopped tomatoes

250g lean sirloin steak, or fillet
steak, trimmed of visible fat

100g watercress

411 Kcal
1718 kJ

"For me, you just can't beat
steak. It helps to give me
the iron and protein I need.
It's a winner every time."

LEE WESTWOOD OBE

Here's a perfect Spanish-style weekend lunch for two that's easy to prepare. As well as being rich in protein, red meat, such as the lean steak used here, is a good source of iron.

Preheat the oven to 220°C/gas mark 7. Toss the sweet potato in 3 tsp oil, paprika and seasoning. Place in a small roasting tin and cook in the oven for 20–25 minutes until golden.

In a small pan, heat the remaining olive oil, fry the garlic and pinch of chilli for a minute, then tip in the tomatoes and heat through.

Preheat the grill. Season the steak. Grill for 4–6 minutes for rare, 8–10 minutes for medium and 10–12 minutes for well done, turning occasionally. Leave to rest for 5 minutes in a warm place, then slice thickly.

Pour the hot tomato mixture over the potatoes and return to the oven for 5 minutes. Tear the watercress in smaller pieces and then arrange the leaves on two serving plates, add the potatoes and top with the sliced steak. Serve with an avocado salad.

SPICED PORK WITH SWEET POTATO & BEAN MASH

SERVES 2 **PREPARE** 10 MINS **COOK** 20-25 MINS

1 pork fillet (about 350g)

1½ tsp ras el hanout spice mix

2 tsp olive oil

400g sweet potato, peeled and cut into chunks

1 small onion, finely chopped

1 stick celery, chopped

2 garlic cloves, crushed

400g can cannellini beans, rinsed and drained

½ tsp chopped fresh lemon thyme, plus extra to garnish

1 tbsp clear honey

594 Kcal
2506 kJ

This is a tasty treat for a weeknight supper with a loved one but it's also special enough to spoil your guests at a dinner party.

Preheat the oven to 200°C/gas mark 6. Trim any fat from the pork and dust with the ras el hanout. Heat 1 teaspoon of the oil in a small frying pan and sear the pork on both sides until browned. Transfer to a small roasting tin and roast in the oven for 20-25 minutes until the fillet is thoroughly cooked and there is no pink meat.

Cook the sweet potato in a pan of boiling water for 10-12 minutes, until tender, then drain well and set aside.

Return the frying pan to the heat with the remaining teaspoon of oil. Add the onion and celery and fry gently for about 5 minutes until very soft, but not browned.

Add the garlic, cannellini beans and cooked sweet potato and scatter with the lemon thyme. Cook very gently for 5 minutes until heated through. Add 3 tablespoons of warm water and crush the bean mixture using a potato masher.

Pile the bean mixture onto warmed serving plates. Cut the pork into chunky slices and arrange on the mash. Stir the honey into the juices left in the tin, then spoon the sauce over the meat. Scatter with extra thyme and serve with strips of griddled courgette.

Note: Green beans make a perfect side for this dish.

MARMALADE & CHILLI-GLAZED DUCK

SERVES 2 **PREPARE** 10 MINS PLUS MARINATING **COOK** 35 MINS

100g reduced-sugar marmalade

Pinch of dried chilli flakes

1 tsp sherry vinegar

Juice of 1 orange

2 duck breasts, skin removed (about 250g)

To serve: orange slices

517 Kcal
2161 kJ

This is a really delicious way of serving duck that's not too heavy, making it an elegant and special dish to cook for two. Duck is sometimes considered fatty but this can be reduced by removing the skin.

In a shallow dish, mix together the marmalade, chilli flakes and sherry vinegar with the orange juice and season lightly. Score the flesh of the duck breasts in a crisscross pattern, then add the duck to the marinade and turn to coat thoroughly in the mixture. Leave to marinate, covered in the fridge, for 1–2 hours.

Preheat the oven to 190°C/gas mark 5. Line a baking tray with parchment paper and transfer the marinated duck breasts onto the tray, spooning the marinade over the top of each one. Place in the oven for about 15 minutes or until cooked, spooning over more marinade a couple of times during the cooking period. Once cooked, let the meat rest for 5 minutes, then cut into thick slices and drizzle over the meat juices. Serve with sliced orange, steamed kale or griddled asparagus and some celeriac or parsnip purée.

Note: You could also use two skinless and boneless chicken breasts instead of the duck.

Serve with Celeriac Chips | page 140 | and a watercress salad as an alternative accompaniment.

PRAWNS WITH GIN & LIME

SERVES 2 **PREPARE** 10 MINS PLUS MARINATING **COOK** 10-12 MINS

20-24 large, peeled
raw king prawns

For the marinade:
2 tbsp gin

2 limes

2 tsp olive oil

Pinch of chilli flakes

1 clove garlic, crushed

A handful of coriander leaves,
chopped (10g)

126 Kcal
531 kJ

This fresh and fragrant dish is yummy served for lunch with the Wild Rice Salad with Orange and Pistachios | page 214 |, a wedge of lemon and the healthy Saffron Yoghurt Aioli | page 226 |.

In a small bowl, mix together the gin, grated zest and juice of 1 lime, the oil, chilli flakes, garlic and coriander. Add the prawns to the marinade, then cover and leave to marinate in the fridge for 3-4 hours or overnight.

Preheat the griddle pan until hot, drain the prawns and place on the griddle and cook for 2-3 minutes until pink, opaque and cooked through. Meanwhile, cut the remaining lime in half and place on the griddle pan for 1-2 minutes each side until heated through. Cut each half in 2 to make 4 wedges.

Serve the prawns with the lime wedges, a watercress salad (or the pomegranate tabbouleh | page 132 |) and spelt bread to soak up the juices with a little Saffron Yoghurt Aioli | page 226 | if you fancy.

Note: For an extra special occasion, when they're in season, you can also marinate lobster or langoustines and griddle to cook through for a luxury starter.

Rachel is a successful businesswoman, co-founding the organic dairy brand Rachel's Organic with her husband.

Her story begins when her sister Dinah survived a heart attack aged 48 – the same age their father died of one. At the same time Rachel's son John, despite enjoying a healthy lifestyle, was also suffering health problems including high blood pressure.

As a dairy farmer and breeder, Rachel had an understanding of genetics, and this led her to thinking that her family might have an inherited condition.

One day she joined Dinah at one of her follow-up appointments and asked the cardiologist if there could be a defective gene in the family. The doctor listened to Rachel's theory and sent her to be tested for familial hypercholesterolaemia (FH), an inherited condition that leads to high cholesterol in the blood from a young age.

The results would take six months to come back, during which time Rachel had more tests including an angiogram. This revealed blocked coronary arteries and she underwent a life-saving coronary artery bypass.

When her test results for FH came back positive it prompted John to have a scan and angiogram, revealing he also had severe coronary heart disease, and he, too, underwent heart bypass surgery.

As Rachel shared her experience with me, it was clear those were difficult days, but without them she fears her son would never have discovered, and been treated for, the life-threatening condition they both have.

Today Rachel takes statins that help control her blood cholesterol. She continues to enjoy a full life, and is now more than ever a firm believer in the benefits of healthy food and plenty of exercise.

CHICKEN & BUTTERNUT SQUASH CURRY

SERVES 2 **PREPARE** 5 MINS **COOK** 30 MINS

1 tbsp vegetable oil

1 onion, sliced

1 clove garlic, crushed

1 cm piece fresh root ginger, peeled and grated

2–3 tsp mild curry powder

300g chicken thigh fillets, cut into chunks

350g diced butternut squash

100g baby spinach

2 tbsp low-fat yoghurt (75g)

To serve: fresh coriander and chopped chillies

Wholewheat chapatis or steamed brown rice

281 Kcal
1182 kJ

Butternut squash has a sweet flavour that goes well with a hint of spice, making it perfect for this quick and warming curry.

Heat half the vegetable oil in a deep frying pan, add the onion, garlic and ginger and gently fry for 5 minutes, or until the onion is very soft but not coloured. Add the curry powder and cook for a minute, then add the remaining oil with the chicken. Fry for 3–4 minutes, before adding the butternut squash, and cook for 1 minute.

Stir in 300ml cold water and mix, then cover with a lid and cook for about 15–20 minutes or until the chicken is cooked through, with no pink meat, and the squash is tender.

Remove from the heat, stir in the spinach, cover and cook until the spinach has wilted. Off the heat, stir in the yoghurt.

Serve the curry with warm wholewheat chapatis or steamed brown basmati rice and top with coriander and extra chopped chillies to suit your taste.

PRAWNS WITH THAI-SPICED BROAD BEANS & WILD RICE

SERVES 2 **PREPARE** 5 MINS **COOK** 25 MINS

125g brown basmati and wild rice

25g Thai green curry paste

400ml homemade chicken stock | page 15 | or ready-made, low-salt alternative

Olive oil spray

1 small onion, finely chopped

1 garlic clove, chopped

1 small red chilli, deseeded and thinly sliced

2–3 cm of fresh root ginger, peeled

100g trimmed fine green beans, cut into 2 cm lengths

30g frozen broad beans, thawed, and (optional) skins removed

A handful of coriander leaves, chopped (10g)

12 raw tiger prawns, peeled

288 Kcal
1204 kJ

Easy to prepare and full of flavour, this Thai-spiced wild rice is a wonderful accompaniment to tiger prawns. Broad beans are a good source of protein, carbohydrates, vitamins and minerals, and brown rice adds fibre. A satisfyingly nutritious dish that makes rice incredibly tasty.

Put the rice, curry paste and stock in a pan and bring to the boil. Cover and simmer for 20–25 minutes.

Meanwhile, spray a frying pan with the oil and cook the onion, garlic, chilli and ginger for about 5 minutes, or until softened. Then stir into the rice mixture and continue cooking until the rice is almost cooked.

Add the green beans and broad beans to the pan, cover and cook for a further 3–4 minutes until the vegetables and rice are tender and all the liquid absorbed. Stir in the coriander.

Meanwhile, return the frying pan to the heat, add the prawns and cook for 3–4 minutes, turning occasionally, until they are opaque and pink all over. Serve the Thai-spiced rice topped with the pan-fried prawns and Roast Cucumber Tzatziki | page 67 |.

Note: For extra flavour, why not try adding some kaffir lime leaf or a lemongrass stick (bruised) to the rice mixture during cooking? Just remember to remove before serving.

VENISON RYE BURGERS WITH CARAMELISED ONION

SERVES 2 **PREPARE** 5 MINS **COOK** 15 MINS

Caramelised onions:

2 tsp olive oil

1 red or white onion, finely sliced

For the burgers:

3 slices (about 1 cm thick)
rye bread

300g minced venison

1 echalion shallot, finely chopped

1 clove garlic, minced

½ tsp dried thyme

1 medium egg yolk

1 tsp vegetable oil

To serve:

1 large tomato, sliced

Little gem lettuce leaves

434 Kcal
1826 kJ

Venison is leaner than other red meats, is a good source of protein and iron and makes a great burger. The caramelised onions give extra flavour to this version, which means you won't need to reach for any sugar-laden sauces.

For the caramelised onions, heat the olive oil in a small saucepan and gently fry the onions, adding a splash of cold water, until they are golden and softened.

Meanwhile, place 1 slice of the rye bread in the food processor and blitz to form fine breadcrumbs, tip into a bowl and set aside.

Mix together the venison mince with the shallot, garlic, thyme, egg yolk and breadcrumbs until evenly combined. Using damp hands, divide the mixture in half and pat into 2 burgers.

Heat the oil in a non-stick frying pan and gently fry for 6–7 minutes on each side or until the burger is cooked through.

Just before serving, toast the remaining 2 slices of rye bread, top each with a slice of tomato, the venison burger, a lettuce leaf and the caramelised onions and Saffron Yoghurt Aioli | page 226 |. Or serve the burgers with Sweet Potato Wedges | page 140 | and a side salad.

VENISON IS LEANER THAN OTHER
RED MEAT, PLUS IT'S A GREAT SOURCE
OF PROTEIN AND IRON

SMOKED CHICKEN & MELON SALAD

SERVES 2 **PREPARE** 20 MINS

½ red onion

1 cantaloupe melon

½ cucumber

120g smoked chicken, cubed

100g cherry plum tomatoes, halved

Large handful flat-leaf parsley
leaves, roughly chopped

Small handful of mint leaves,
roughly chopped

Large handful of curly lettuce
or frisée

For the vinaigrette:
3 raspberries

3 tbsp extra virgin olive oil

1 tbsp red wine vinegar

1 tsp clear honey

1 tsp chopped tarragon leaves

378 Kcal
1578 kJ

This salad makes a lovely centrepiece for a romantic picnic.
The smoked chicken adds a lot of flavour but it is salty, so take
care with how much you use – I've tweaked the proportions
to get the balance just right.

Thinly slice the red onion and place in a bowl of ice-cold water,
then set aside. Cut the melon in half, discard the seeds and carefully
scoop out the flesh. Chop 250g of the melon flesh into bite-sized
chunks (keeping the remaining flesh for use in fruit salads or
smoothies). Keep the melon shells to use as bowls. Level off the
base of the melon shells to sit neatly on a surface.

Peel and deseed the cucumber and cut into chunks. Drain the
onions and combine with the cucumber and the remaining
salad ingredients.

To make the vinaigrette, crush the raspberries in a bowl with
the back of a spoon, then combine with the remaining dressing
ingredients and season with black pepper. Toss with the salad
and mix everything together.

Note: This recipe would also work well with any smoked meat or fish.

LAMB WITH ROASTED CUMIN CAULIFLOWER

SERVES 2 **PREPARE** 10 MINS **COOK** 25 MINS

1 cauliflower,
cut into florets

1 tbsp olive oil

1½ tsp ground cumin

½ tsp caraway seeds,
lightly crushed

1 red onion, sliced

2 lamb leg steaks,
trimmed of visible fat

Black pepper

Lemon juice

To serve: A handful of
parsley, chopped (10g)

382 Kcal
1598 kJ

If you've never tried roasting cauliflower before, you won't look back after this! Lamb has a higher fat content than poultry but that doesn't mean you have to exclude it from your diet completely. By choosing lean cuts and trimming off any fat, you can still enjoy it every now and then.

Preheat the oven to 200°C/gas mark 6. Blanch the cauliflower in boiling water for 3–4 minutes and drain.

Meanwhile, place the oil in a roasting tin with the spices and sliced onion and roast for 5 minutes. Then toss the blanched cauliflower in the hot spiced oil, return to the oven and roast for 15–20 minutes, until the cauliflower is cooked.

Season the lamb with black pepper and cook under a hot grill for 4–5 minutes each side or until cooked to your liking. Squeeze over the lemon juice, serve with the roasted cauliflower and garnish with the chopped parsley.

Note: Try serving with a spoonful of Baba Ganoush | page 72 | or Roasted Cucumber Tzatziki | page 67 |.

TRY SERVING WITH A SPOONFUL
OF BABA GANOUSH (PAGE 72)

LESS SALT. MORE FLAVOUR.

Reducing your intake of salt is important for a healthy heart as too much, too often is linked to high blood pressure. Swap seasoning with salt for adding herbs, chilli or dried spices for that extra flavour punch.

VEAL ESCALOPES WITH THYME, MUSTARD & LENTILS

SERVES 2 **PREPARE** 10 MINS **COOK** 30 MINS

50g red split lentils

3 sprigs of thyme

2 tbsp olive oil

1 echalion shallot, finely sliced
(about 100g)

2 plum tomatoes, diced
(about 250g)

1 tsp Dijon mustard

200ml homemade chicken stock
or vegetable stock | page 15 |
or ready-made, low-salt alternative

115g pack fresh spinach

2 veal escalopes (about 150g each)

220g tenderstem broccoli,
ends trimmed

451 Kcal
1888 kJ

This flavour-filled combination is quick to cook, making it ideal for a healthy weekday supper with company. The subtle flavour of the veal gets a boost from the thyme and mustard-infused lentils.

Rinse the lentils thoroughly in a large bowl of cold water. Drain and set aside. Pull the leaves from the thyme stalks and set aside.

Heat 1 tbsp oil and gently fry the shallot for 2 minutes until soft, then add the tomatoes and fry for a further 2 minutes. Add the thyme, mustard, stock and lentils and simmer for 15 minutes, or until the lentils are tender.

Stir in the spinach and allow to wilt. Season the veal with black pepper and a sprinkle of thyme. Heat the remaining oil in a non-stick frying pan and fry the veal for 4–5 minutes, or until cooked. Meanwhile, steam or boil the broccoli for 3–4 minutes. Serve with the lentils.

SEA BASS PARCEL WITH MED VEG

SERVES 2 **PREPARE** 10 MINS **COOK** 15 MINS

150g baby new potatoes, halved

1 courgette, thinly sliced

2 peppers – 1 orange and 1 yellow, deseeded and diced

2 sea bass fillets (about 200g)

A handful of flat-leaf parsley, leaves picked (10g)

1 tsp olive oil

½ lemon, cut into 2 wedges

Dressing, to serve:
2 tbsp extra virgin olive oil or avocado oil

1 small clove garlic, peeled and sliced

7g pine nuts, lightly toasted

Juice of ½ lemon

1 tbsp capers, rinsed and drained (about 25g)

A small handful of fresh basil, finely chopped (about 5g)

369 Kcal
1542 kJ

This simple fish dish is a great recipe for a spring date and you can have it on the table in less than half an hour. Quicker than ordering a takeaway and good for your heart too!

Preheat the oven to 220°C/gas mark 7. Cook the potatoes in a saucepan of boiling water for about 10 minutes, until tender.

Divide the courgettes and peppers between 2 large squares of foil. Place a sea bass fillet on top of each and season. Bring up the edges of the foil and tightly seal. Sit the parcels on a baking sheet and bake for 15 minutes, until the fish is cooked through and the vegetables are tender.

Meanwhile, whisk together the dressing ingredients. Drain the potatoes and return to the pan. Add the parsley and olive oil and toss well together. Serve with the fish, vegetables and any cooking juices with the dressing drizzled over and serve.

SUMMERY CRAB LINGUINE

SERVES 2 **PREPARE** 10 MINS **COOK** 15 MINS

2 tbsp extra virgin olive oil

1 garlic clove, finely chopped

1 red chilli, deseeded and finely chopped

1 echalion shallot, finely chopped

100g dried wholewheat linguine

Splash of white wine or prosecco (optional)

100g white crab meat

Grated zest and juice of ½ lemon

Handful flat-leaf parsley, chopped

Handful dill, chopped

354 Kcal
1485 kJ

This stylish dish is enough for a starter for four or a light lunch for two. The sweet white crab meat, zesty lemon, chilli and garlic cling to the strands of pasta, making a really flavour-filled sauce – important when you're cooking without salt.

Using wholewheat pasta helps to up the fibre content of this dish and, if you serve it with plenty of salad or some griddled vegetables on the side, it'll go towards your five a day as well.

Heat 1 tbsp oil in a frying pan over a medium heat. Add the garlic, chilli and shallot and cook for about 10 minutes until soft and starting to turn golden.

Meanwhile, cook the pasta in boiling water according to the pack instructions, then drain, reserving a cupful of the cooking liquid.

Add the wine (if using) to the garlic mixture and simmer until almost evaporated, then tip in the pasta with a little cooking liquid and toss to coat. Take off the heat and stir through the crab, lemon zest and juice, then season. Stir through the herbs and drizzle with the remaining 1 tbsp oil, then serve at once.

"Pasta and seafood are two of my favourites and this dish has plenty of fibre and tasty crab meat. Great for when I'm training and need to keep my energy up. I have it with lots of veg or salad – as an athlete it's important that I get at least five a day. I often end up having five with every meal!"

DAME SARAH STOREY

ROASTED AUBERGINE & GOAT'S CHEESE PASTA

SERVES 2 **PREPARE** 10 MINS **COOK** 40-45 MINS

1 medium aubergine, cut into wedges

1 red onion, cut into wedges

2 cloves garlic, finely chopped

2 tbsp extra virgin olive oil

250g cherry tomatoes or large tomatoes, quartered

8 leaves fresh basil, shredded, plus a few whole leaves for garnishing

150g wholemeal spaghetti or fusilli

75g creamy goat's cheese

529 Kcal
2200 kJ

This dish has a yummy, garlicky flavour that tastes just as good the next day. The flavour is enhanced by the tangy goat's cheese – which should be used sparingly to avoid too much saturated fat and salt.

Preheat the oven to 200°C/gas mark 6. Arrange the aubergine and onion in a small roasting tin. Scatter over the chopped garlic, and drizzle with the olive oil. Roast for 30–35 minutes, stirring once or twice. When tender and charred, add the tomatoes and basil leaves and cook for a further 10 minutes or until the tomatoes are soft and their skins are splitting.

Meanwhile, bring a large pan of water to the boil and cook the pasta for 8 minutes or until tender. Drain and toss with the cooked vegetables, goat's cheese and seasoning. Garnish with basil leaves and serve with a watercress salad dressed with a little balsamic vinegar.

Note: You can also scatter with toasted hazelnuts as a garnish before serving.

RUSSELL'S STORY

As a young man Russell had a huge passion for sport, something I can relate to.

A keen football and tennis player, he also swam, ran, and loved to go wind and kite surfing.

Aged just 23, he suffered a heart attack whilst kite surfing. Since he was living such a healthy lifestyle it came out of the blue, leaving him with reduced heart muscle function.

Russell was diagnosed with coronary heart disease and needed a year of recuperation. But recuperate he did – and, to mark the 10th anniversary of his heart attack, he planned to raise £10,000 for the BHF, taking part in a series of swimming, cycling and triathlon events to achieve his target.

Twelve years after his heart attack, Russell suffered a stroke at work and spent the next few weeks learning how to walk again. He is now back to running, swimming and cycling.

Spending time with Russell confirmed to me what his inspiring story suggests, that he is someone whose mental strength matches his athletic ability.

To this day there is no explanation as to why Russell developed coronary heart disease at such a young age. Though he still struggles with his speech, he is determined that his health problems will not prevent him from doing the things he loves, such as playing sport and enjoying life with his wife Rachel.

I heart hosting. Whether it's drinks and nibbles, an intimate dinner with close friends, or catering for a big crowd, every host or hostess needs some tried and tested recipes to indulge and delight their guests.

If you're trying to eat well and look after your heart you might think these sorts of gatherings are best avoided, but that needn't be the case.

The following recipes offer a healthier choice compared to standard dishes, leaving your guests feeling satisfied and coming back for more.

And like all good entertaining dishes, these recipes are easy to make, so you can prepare ahead and enjoy being with friends and family, rather than spending all your time in the kitchen.

SALMON-TOPPED SPELT & BEETROOT BLINIS

MAKES 18-20 (1 PER SERVING) **PREPARE** 10 MINS **COOK** 10 MINS

50g spelt flour

½ tsp baking powder

2 eggs, beaten

100g fresh raw beetroot, coarsely grated

Sunflower oil cooking spray

For the topping:

½ cucumber peeled, deseeded

3 tbsp half-fat crème fraîche

20g dill, chopped

140g smoked salmon

44 Kcal
184 kJ

Beetroot and smoked salmon are the ideal flavour and colour combination for this party canapé. Spelt and beetroot blini bases make a healthier alternative to classic ones, plus they have more flavour!

For lunch or a starter, you can make 6–8 larger blinis. In this case, use 3–4 tablespoons of the beetroot mix and cook for 2–3 minutes on each side before topping with the crème fraîche and smoked salmon.

Place the flour in a large bowl with the baking powder, make a well in the centre and pour in the eggs. Mix together to form a thick paste, then stir in the beetroot.

Spray a non-stick frying pan with the oil and spoon in small rounds of the mixture. Cook for 1–2 minutes before turning and cooking for a further minute. Continue in batches, keeping the cooked fritters warm as you go, until all the mixture is used.

For the topping, cut the cucumber into very small cubes and dry on kitchen paper to remove excess water. Mix with the crème fraîche and dill. Spoon a little onto each of the fritters and top with a piece of smoked salmon.

Note: It can be tempting to spoon too much mixture into the pan for each blini but they expand while cooking so keep them small.

The smoking process means that the smoked salmon contains more salt. Watch how much you add and save it for those special occasions.

As an alternative topping, try the Homemade Houmous | page 73 | and some fresh coriander leaves.

CUCUMBER BLINIS WITH GOAT'S CHEESE & TOMATO

MAKES 24 (1 PER SERVING) **PREPARE** 10 MINS **COOK** 20 MINS

18 cherry tomatoes,
cut in half

1 tbsp olive oil

Half a cucumber

100g soft goat's cheese

24 sprigs thyme, to garnish

Balsamic pearls, to garnish
(optional)

15 Kcal
64 kJ

These blinis are a lighter choice, using cucumber as the base of the canapé. Just halve or double the recipe depending on how many people are coming over.

Preheat the oven to 180°C/gas mark 4. Arrange the tomatoes on a small tray, drizzle over the olive oil and roast for about 20 minutes, until they have softened.

Using a vegetable peeler, remove strips of peel lengthways in alternate stripes down the outside of the cucumber. Then slice into 1 cm thick slices, and arrange on a plate. Spoon a little of the goat's cheese on each of the cucumber slices and top with the roasted tomato halves and a sprig of thyme. Serve garnished with balsamic pearls.

SALMON-TOPPED SPELT &
BEETROOT BLINIS (PAGE 194)

BACON, LETTUCE & TOMATO
BITES (PAGE 198)

CUCUMBER BLINIS WITH GOAT'S
CHEESE & TOMATO (PAGE 195)

BACON, LETTUCE & TOMATO BITES

MAKES ABOUT 20 (1 PER SERVING) **PREPARE** 25 MINS **COOK** 8 MINS

75g cubed smoked pancetta

20 baby plum tomatoes
(about 400g)

Few handfuls round lettuce
leaves, stalks removed

1-2 tbsp reduced-fat mayonnaise

¼ tsp chipotle paste

16 Kcal
67 kJ

It's hard not to like so many flavours in one bite. Not only do these stuffed plum tomato bites look elegant, they are also light and really easy to make. The chipotle mayonnaise adds a delicious depth.

Place a large frying pan over a medium heat. Fry the pancetta for 6–8 minutes until golden. Lift out of the pan with a slotted spoon, blot dry on kitchen paper and allow to cool.

Trim a thin slice from the base of each tomato, so they sit upright. Then slice the tops off the tomatoes and, using a teaspoon, scoop the flesh from the tomato cups and discard. Place the scooped-out tomatoes upside-down on kitchen paper to drain any excess liquid.

Place the mayonnaise in a small bowl and stir in the chipotle paste, mixing well.

Fold a small piece of lettuce in half and push it down inside the tomato to line the bottom, leaving a little of the lettuce peeking out of the top of the tomato. Fill the tomatoes with the cooked pancetta and finish with a small dot of the chipotle mayonnaise.

YOGHURT CREATES A CREAMY SAUCE
WITHOUT LOTS OF SATURATED FAT

WATERCRESS PESTO

SERVES 4 **PREPARE** 10 MINS

1 clove garlic, peeled

6 tbsp extra virgin olive oil

30g freshly grated
Parmigiano Reggiano

200g watercress, coarsely chopped

200g natural low-fat yoghurt

Lemon juice to taste

 220 Kcal
909 kJ

This is a peppery version of the traditional basil pesto. It's lovely to stir into pasta for a quick and easy lunch with some salad, and the yoghurt gives you a creamy sauce without lots of saturated fat.

Place the garlic and olive oil in a food processor with the Parmigiano Reggiano, then whizz briefly until coarsely chopped and blended. Gradually add the watercress, pulsing briefly until chopped.

Add the yoghurt and give the mixture another quick whizz to form a coarse purée. Season generously with ground black pepper and lemon juice to taste. Spoon into a jar and chill. This will keep in an airtight container in the fridge for 1–2 days. Perfect as a dip with vegetable batons.

CHARGRILLED ASPARAGUS & BROCCOLI WITH FETA

SERVES 4 **PREPARE** 10 MINS **COOK** 10 MINS

1 tsp olive oil

1 clove garlic, crushed

230g asparagus, woody
ends trimmed

250g tenderstem broccoli, trimmed

40g light Greek-style salad cheese

1 tsp cumin seeds, toasted

2 tbsp roughly chopped mint

Grated zest and juice of ½ lemon

1 tbsp pumpkin seeds, toasted

 120 Kcal
501 kJ

Warm or cold, this salad is nutritious and completely satisfying.
I particularly love the flavour of the toasted cumin seeds and the
nuttiness of the pumpkin seeds. Even though the British asparagus
season is short, it's worth the wait.

Add the olive oil and garlic to the asparagus and tenderstem broccoli
spears and toss to coat. Heat a griddle pan or barbecue, and cook
the broccoli and asparagus for 6–8 minutes, turning frequently, until
tender and slightly charred. You may need to do this in 2 batches.

Meanwhile, crumble the cheese into a bowl and mix with the cumin
seeds, chopped mint, lemon zest and juice.

Serve the chargrilled asparagus and broccoli between four plates
and scatter over the cheese mixture. Grind over plenty of black
pepper and serve sprinkled with the pumpkin seeds.

Note: Sprinkle with freshly sliced red chilli or chilli flakes for an
added kick.

I was shocked to discover
that coronary heart disease
is the UK's single biggest
killer, which is why I wanted
to work with the BHF to raise
awareness of heart health,
and help raise vital funds for
research through challenges
such as the BHF's London to
Brighton Bike Ride.

VENISON WITH BLUEBERRY SAUCE

SERVES 4 **PREPARE** 10 MINS **COOK** 25 MINS

1 tbsp oil

4 venison steaks
(about 125–150g each)

A pinch of crushed pink
peppercorns or ground
black pepper

*For the soured cream
and celeriac mash:*
800g celeriac, peeled

10g sunflower spread

100ml reduced-fat soured cream

A handful of fresh dill or chives,
chopped (10g), plus extra
for garnish

Zest of ½ lemon and 1 tbsp juice

For the blueberry sauce:
200ml red wine

350g blueberries

295 Kcal
1238 kJ

Blueberries are perfect for adding to cereal or porridge, but they are
also delicious in lesser-known recipes like this one. Blueberries and
venison are an unusual pairing that nods to Nordic cuisine.

Cut the celeriac into chunks and cook in a pan of boiling water for
10–15 minutes until tender. Meanwhile, heat the oil in a frying pan.
Season the venison with the pepper and fry gently for 6–8 minutes
for medium, turning occasionally. Add 150ml wine and reduce by
half. Remove the steaks and keep warm.

When the celeriac is tender, drain thoroughly and return to the pan.
Add the sunflower spread and soured cream, and mash the celeriac.
Stir in the dill or chives, lemon juice and zest and season well.

Add the blueberries to the pan with the reduced wine. Pour in the
remaining wine and cook for 3–4 minutes until the blueberries start
to burst, then season.

Slice the steaks and serve on top of the mash with the blueberry
sauce spooned over and garnish with dill or chives.

MISO BEEF WITH SOY MUSTARD SAUCE

SERVES 6 **PREPARE** 20 MINS PLUS MARINATING **COOK** 35 MINS

800g beef fillet

2 tbsp olive oil

2 tbsp sesame seeds

For the miso marinade:
3 tbsp sake

3 tbsp mirin

150g sweet white miso

75g caster sugar

1 tbsp English mustard

For the soy mustard sauce:
2 tbsp English mustard powder

1 tbsp Japanese rice vinegar

2 tbsp reduced-sodium soy sauce

125ml dry white wine

2 tbsp white wine vinegar

1 tsp lemon juice

1 shallot, quartered

200ml half-fat crème fraîche

327 Kcal
1367 kJ

This is a special dish for entertaining – it's never left a guest disappointed. By choosing lean meat, like this beef fillet, you can enjoy the benefits of red meat but without the saturated fat and salt that are sometimes found in its processed counterparts.

For the marinade, heat all the ingredients in a pan over a medium heat until the sugar has dissolved. Cool, then tip into a resealable freezer bag; add the beef. Chill for anything between 4–48 hours. The longer it marinates, the tastier it will be.

To make the sauce, mix the mustard powder with 1 tbsp cold water to form a paste. Add the rice vinegar and soy sauce, then mix together until smooth; set aside.

In a small pan, heat the wine, white wine vinegar, lemon juice and shallot, simmer until reduced and syrupy, then remove and discard the shallot. Remove from the heat and stir in the crème fraîche and the soy mustard mixture.

Preheat the oven to 200°C/gas mark 6. Remove the beef from the marinade and wipe off any excess with kitchen paper. Heat the olive oil in a frying pan over a medium-high heat and sear the beef for 1–2 minutes on each side, then transfer to a roasting tray and place in the oven for 20 minutes (for medium-rare). Set aside to rest for at least 15 minutes.

Dry-toast the sesame seeds in a frying pan until golden. Slice the beef, spoon over a little sauce and scatter over the sesame seeds. Serve with sticky rice and pak choi, if liked.

CAULIFLOWER CHEESE & SPINACH BAKES

SERVES 4 **PREPARE** 5 MINS **COOK** 40 MINS

15g unsaturated spread,
plus extra for greasing
(e.g. sunflower spread)

15g plain flour

300ml skimmed milk

40g reduced-fat mature strong
cheddar-style cheese, grated

700g whole cauliflower, trimmed
and cut into small florets

115g fresh spinach, chopped

1–2 tsp English mustard powder

1 shallot, finely chopped

4 egg whites

2 tbsp chives to garnish

 223 Kcal
932 kJ

A cheese bake might sound indulgent but small changes, like using skimmed milk and reduced-fat cheese, quickly transform this into a lower-fat option for light lunches or starters.

Preheat the oven to 200°C/gas mark 6. Grease 4×350ml (or 2×1 litre) ramekins or soufflé dishes. Melt the unsaturated spread in a pan, stir in the flour and return to the heat for 30 seconds to 1 minute. Remove from the heat and gradually stir in the milk, a little at a time, making sure that the milk is fully incorporated between each addition. Stir in the cheese, return the pan to the heat and bring back to the boil, stirring continuously. Remove from the heat and allow to cool.

Meanwhile, cook the cauliflower in a pan of boiling water for 10–15 minutes, until very soft. Drain well, then roughly mash. Add the chopped spinach into the cauliflower mash. Mix in the cheese sauce, mustard powder and shallot. Season with black pepper.

In a large bowl, whisk the egg whites until they form stiff peaks. Using a large metal spoon, gently fold into the cauliflower mixture. Then spoon this mixture into the prepared dishes and bake for 20–25 minutes, until well risen and golden brown. Serve straight away.

PORK WITH SPICY PLUM SAUCE

SERVES 6 **PREPARE** 10 MINS PLUS MARINATING **COOK** 20 MINS

2 pork fillets (about 800g)

1 shallot, roughly chopped

10g parsley

Grated zest and juice of 1 lemon

2 tsp rapeseed oil

For the plum sauce:

1 tbsp olive oil

1 large onion, chopped

2 cloves garlic, finely chopped

2 red chillies, deseeded
and finely chopped

1 tsp mustard seeds

600g plums, stoned and chopped

1 tbsp clear honey or agave syrup

1 tsp ground allspice

2 tbsp white wine vinegar

239 Kcal
1003 kJ

These unusual flavour combinations bring something a little different to your dinner party. The plum sauce is almost chutney-like and full of flavour.

Begin by making the plum sauce. Heat the oil in a pan and cook the onion, garlic, chilli and mustard seeds for 5 minutes or until softened. Add the plums, honey, allspice and vinegar and simmer together for 15–20 minutes until pulpy and juicy.

Trim the visible fat from the pork. Place the shallot and parsley in a mini blender and whizz until finely chopped. Add the lemon zest, lemon juice and 2 tbsp water and whizz again to make a coarse paste. Pour over the pork in a shallow dish and roll the fillets to coat in the marinade. Leave for 5–10 minutes.

Preheat the oven to 200°C/gas mark 6 and preheat the griddle pan with the rapeseed oil. Lift the pork out of the marinade, shake off any excess and cook for 2–3 minutes on each side until golden, then transfer to a roasting tin and roast for a further 25–30 minutes, or until cooked through.

Serve with the sauce and Wild Rice Salad with Orange and Pistachios | page 214 | or chargrilled tenderstem broccoli or wilted Swiss chard.

WILD RICE SALAD WITH ORANGE & PISTACHIOS

SERVES 6 **PREPARE** 10 MINS **COOK** 30 MINS

450g mixed brown and wild rice

300g broad beans, double podded

Grated zest and juice of 1 orange

Bunch of spring onions, trimmed
and finely chopped

50g pistachios

100g wild rocket

 366 Kcal
1530 kJ

This wholesome salad is the perfect accompaniment to grilled meat or fish and works well as part of a buffet or barbecue.

Both brown and wild rice contain fibre, while the broad beans, onions and rocket mean you are well on the way towards your five a day. You can replace the rocket with chopped spinach and combine different herbs or edible flowers. I also add a couple of drops of Tabasco for a spicy kick.

Preheat the oven to 170°C/gas mark 3. Cook the rice in a large pan of water for about 25 minutes. Add the beans and cook for a further 2–3 minutes, until the beans and the rice are tender and cooked.

Drain well and tip into a large serving bowl. Add the orange zest, juice and spring onions and leave to cool.

Meanwhile, spread the pistachios out on a baking sheet and cook for 10 minutes, or until golden. Remove from the oven and allow to cool before roughly chopping. Then fold through the rice salad with the rocket leaves, season to taste and serve.

Note: When in season, replace the broad beans with steamed asparagus spears, cut into 2 cm lengths.

Instead of stirring through, the pistachios look elegant when sprinkled on top.

WARM SEARED BEEF & PEA SHOOT SALAD

SERVES 4 **PREPARE** 10 MINS **COOK** 70 MINS

2 red onions, cut into 8-10 wedges

300g small beetroots, scrubbed and cut into quarters

2 tbsp olive oil

3½ tbsp balsamic vinegar

1–2 sprigs rosemary, leaves only, roughly chopped

1 tsp groundnut oil

4×150g beef fillet steaks

2 large handfuls of rocket or pea shoots (70g)

1 tbsp sesame seeds, toasted (15g – optional)

Parmigiano Reggiano shavings (optional)

306 Kcal
1281 kJ

This might take a little while to cook but it's easy to prepare and perfect for some leisurely cooking at the weekend.

The fillet steaks used in this recipe are lean, which means that the excess saturated fat found in fattier cuts of meat is avoided.

Preheat the oven to 200°C/gas mark 6. Arrange the onions and beetroots in a roasting tray into which they just fit comfortably. Mix together the olive oil, half the vinegar and rosemary. Season. Pour over the onions and beetroot. Stir well to coat, loosely cover with a piece of foil to stop them burning but don't seal the dish.

Roast for 25 minutes, then turn and baste well, adding 1–2 tbsp water if it looks dry. Return to the oven for 25 minutes, then baste again and cook for a further 15 minutes without the foil or until soft and caramelised.

When the beetroot and onions are nearly cooked, heat a griddle pan until very hot and brush with the groundnut oil. Remove and discard all visible fat from the steaks, then season with black pepper and sear for 2 minutes a side (or longer depending on how you like your steaks cooked). Transfer the steaks onto a plate, cover and keep warm. Leave to rest for 4–5 minutes before thinly slicing.

Arrange the rocket over a serving plate, top with the caramelised onions and beetroot, then the seared sliced steak. Drizzle over the cooking juices mixed with the rest of the balsamic vinegar. Serve scattered with the sesame seeds and Parmesan shavings if you wish.

Note: If beetroots are not in season and sweet when making this dish, then try the ready-cooked vacuum-packed versions (not in vinegar).

USING LEAN FILLET STEAKS HELPS
TO LIMIT THE SATURATED FAT

MARINATED SALMON WITH STIR-FRIED VEG & SPELT

SERVES 4 **PREPARE** 5 MINS PLUS MARINATING **COOK** 15 MINS

1–2 tbsp light soy sauce

2 tbsp mirin

1 lemongrass stalk, split and bruised

2–3 cm piece fresh root ginger, grated

4 salmon fillets (about 560g)

250g pouch cooked mixed grains, such as spelt, quinoa, red and wild rice mix

1 tbsp olive oil

2 cloves garlic, crushed

3–4 spring onions, sliced

100g tenderstem broccoli, cut into smaller florets

100g small courgettes, trimmed and thinly sliced

150g sugar snap peas, cut in half lengthways

100g pack baby spinach

To serve: yuzu juice or wedges of lime

Chilli flakes

372 Kcal
1558 kJ

As well as being easy to prepare, this recipe is rich in omega-3 fatty acids and fibre. It provides one of your two recommended weekly portions of fish.

In a small shallow bowl, mix the soy sauce and mirin with the lemongrass stalk. Gather the grated ginger in your hands and squeeze out the ginger juice into the soy mixture. Finally, dry the salmon fillets with kitchen paper, then place flesh side down in the bowl and leave to marinate for 15 minutes or longer, covered in the fridge.

Preheat the oven to 180°C/gas mark 4. Remove the salmon from the marinade, reserving the marinade, then place the salmon (skin side up) on a baking sheet lined with non-stick baking parchment. Bake for 10–15 minutes until just cooked.

Meanwhile, heat a wok or large frying pan, tip in the pouch of mixed grains and pan-fry for 2–3 minutes before spooning onto a plate and setting aside. Return the pan to the heat with the oil, add the garlic and spring onions and stir-fry for 1–2 minutes until slightly softened. Add the tenderstem broccoli, courgettes and sugar snap peas and cook for 2–3 minutes, adding a splash of water halfway through cooking. Continue to cook until the vegetables are just softening. Return the mixed grains to the pan.

Discard the lemongrass from the reserved marinade and add to the pan. Bring the marinade to the boil and then stir through the grain mix with the spinach. Serve the salmon whole or, if you prefer, broken into large chunky flakes.

SIMON'S STORY

Simon's career as a chef took him all over Europe. When he returned to the UK he swapped the kitchen for the classroom, becoming Head of Catering at Leicester College.

At the age of 46, Simon collapsed while coaching the local primary school football team. Tests revealed he had dilated cardiomyopathy, the same heart condition that had caused his father's sudden death aged just 44.

As it's usually an inherited condition, Simon made sure his own children were tested and was relieved when all three were given the all-clear.

After his diagnosis Simon was fitted with a pacemaker and returned home determined to live life to the full. He bought a motorbike, took up gardening, and even coached the school football team to victory in the local cup.

But his condition worsened and, following another collapse, he was fitted with a combined pacemaker and ICD – which would also help his heart to pump more efficiently – and given the distressing news that he only had 12 months to live.

With his health deteriorating, Simon was put on a transplant list and in 2005 underwent a successful, life-saving operation.

When Simon shared his story with me it was clear he felt incredibly lucky to have been given a second chance, one he wasn't going to waste. Following the transplant, he made it his mission to make the most of his new life and achieve his lifelong goals.

One such ambition was to reintroduce honey bees into his village, which he fulfilled in spades, ending up not only with 90 hives, but his own beekeeping business employing five people.

QUICK SEAFOOD PAELLA

SERVES 4 **PREPARE** 10 MINS **COOK** 20–25 MINS

1 tsp olive oil

1 onion, thinly sliced

2 red peppers, thinly sliced

3 cloves garlic, finely chopped

250g paella rice

Pinch of saffron

2 tsp sweet smoked paprika

227g can chopped tomatoes

600–800ml hot homemade chicken stock | page 15 | or ready-made, low-salt alternative

200g trimmed fine green beans, cut into 4 cm lengths

150g peeled raw king prawns

125g squid, cut into rings

200g cod, or other white fish, cut into chunks

25g flat-leaf parsley, chopped

391 Kcal
1656 kJ

Surprisingly speedy to make, this classic Spanish dish is ideal for long summer evenings with friends. To get a head start you can prepare all the ingredients and fry the onions, pepper and garlic in advance, so you can be ready to go when your guests arrive.

Heat the olive oil in a large pan and gently fry the onion, peppers and garlic for 5 minutes, or until they have softened.

Stir in the rice, saffron and paprika, and cook for a few seconds before stirring in the chopped tomatoes and the hot stock. Leave on a medium heat for about 15 minutes, covered, stirring occasionally. When the rice is nearly done and most – but not all – of the stock is absorbed, add the beans. Stir in the prawns, squid and cod, and heat for a further 5–6 minutes or until the rice is tender and the prawns are pink in colour, cooked through and piping hot.

Stir in the chopped parsley and serve with wedges of lemon to squeeze over, and a spoonful of Saffron Yoghurt Aioli | page 226 | if you like.

Note: Sometimes I add a handful of fresh or frozen peas towards the end of cooking. I also like to add a dollop of natural low-fat Greek-style yoghurt and some fresh chillies.

SPANISH FISH & CHORIZO STEW

SERVES 4 **PREPARE** 5 MINS **COOK** 20 MINS

80g cooking chorizo

1 tsp olive oil

2 cloves garlic, crushed

1 onion, thinly sliced

1 red pepper, sliced

2 tsp sweet smoked paprika

400g can chickpeas, drained and rinsed

100ml dry sherry or 50ml sherry vinegar

900g fresh plum tomatoes, roughly chopped

Sprig of rosemary

115g fresh spinach

600g skinless, boneless monkfish or hake fillets

To serve: flat-leaf parsley

Saffron Yoghurt Aioli | page 226 |

328 Kcal
1376 kJ

This vibrant stew is warming and hearty, with the traditional Spanish flavours of paprika, sherry and chorizo.

Although it's high in salt and fat, a little chorizo goes a long way and I was delighted we could keep some in this recipe. Using a small amount combined with smoked paprika makes a huge difference to the flavour.

Cut the chorizo into small dice and add to a sauté or deep frying pan with the oil. Fry for 2–3 minutes, until the chorizo is cooked and its lovely red oil is released. Add the garlic, onion and pepper and fry gently for a further 4–5 minutes, or until softened.

Add the paprika and cook for 30 seconds before stirring in the chickpeas and the sherry. Return to the heat and bring it to the boil. Then add the chopped tomatoes and the sprig of rosemary. Cover and reduce the heat and allow to simmer for 4–5 minutes until the tomatoes are softened. Remove the lid and simmer for a further 2–3 minutes so that the sauce thickens.

Stir in the spinach and then place the fish on top of the stew, cover and leave to cook for 5 minutes, or until the fish is cooked and opaque white in colour. Garnish with a little chopped parsley and serve with a generous spoonful of the Saffron Yoghurt Aioli.

Note: You can also serve with a griddled triangle of sourdough bread to soak up the juices.

SERVE WITH A GENEROUS
SPOONFUL OF SAFFRON
YOGHURT AIOLI (PAGE 226)

SAFFRON YOGHURT AIOLI

MAKES 150ML (SERVES 4) **PREPARE** 5 MINS

Small pinch saffron threads

150g natural low-fat yoghurt or skyr

1 clove garlic, crushed (optional)

Squeeze of lemon juice

22 Kcal
92 kJ

You only need four ingredients and five minutes to make this delicious recipe. Lower in salt and fat than a traditional mayonnaise-based aioli, it really lifts the Quick Seafood Paella | page 222 |, the Spanish Fish and Chorizo Stew | page 224 | and breakfast egg dishes, such as Eggs Florentine | page 39 |.

Place the saffron threads in a bowl and cover with 2 tbsp boiling water. Leave to soak and infuse for 5 minutes.

Stir in the yoghurt with the garlic, if using, a squeeze of lemon juice and season to taste.

CORN & CHILLI SLAW

SERVES 12 **PREPARE** 30 MINS **COOK** 10 MINS

125g canned sweetcorn,
drained

4 carrots, shredded
or coarsely grated

1 red cabbage, core and outer
leaves removed and shredded

4 red chillies (or 2 red peppers)
deseeded and sliced

300ml reduced-fat soured cream

1 tbsp red wine vinegar

Juice of 2 limes and zest of 1

1 tsp Dijon mustard

A bunch of fresh coriander,
roughly chopped (25g)

1 avocado, chopped

 328 Kcal
1371 kJ

This fresh and colourful slaw is a great pairing with the Pulled Pork and Sweet Potato Chilli | page 228 | or other barbecued meats.

In a preheated non-stick frying pan, dry-fry the sweetcorn kernels for about 3–4 minutes and set aside.

Toss the carrots, cabbage and red chillies (or red peppers) together in a large bowl. Stir in the soured cream, vinegar, lime juice, zest and mustard and season. Pour over the vegetables and toss together. Chill in the fridge until needed.

Just before serving, toss again, adding the coriander, and scatter over the charred sweetcorn and chopped avocado. Garnish with lime wedges and serve.

Note: Shredding your vegetables as thinly as possible will make this vibrant slaw even more appealing.

PULLED PORK & SWEET POTATO CHILLI

SERVES 12 **PREPARE** 30 MINS **COOK** 3 HOURS 15 MINS

1 tbsp olive oil

1.5kg pork shoulder steaks

2 onions, sliced

4 cloves garlic, sliced

2 green chillies, chopped

1 tbsp molasses sugar

1 tsp ground cumin

1 tsp dried oregano

½ tsp sweet smoked paprika

¼ tsp chilli powder

½ tsp ground coriander

Pinch of ground cloves

1 cinnamon stick

2×400g cans peeled plum tomatoes

500ml homemade chicken stock | page 15 | or ready-made, low-salt alternative

Juice of 1 orange

Juice of 2 limes

500g sweet potatoes, peeled

2×400g cans kidney beans

Handful coriander leaves

315 Kcal
1317 kJ

We've given this indulgent smash-hit a healthy makeover. The high salt, sugar and saturated fat content of traditional pulled pork is minimised by using plenty of herbs and spices for flavour.

Served with brown basmati rice and the Corn and Chilli Slaw | page 227 |, this will have them coming back for second helpings. Sometimes I add chopped red chillies for extra punch.

Heat the oil in a large casserole pan over a medium-high heat. Season the steaks and add to the pan, browning on each side (you may need to do this in batches). Set aside.

Lower the heat slightly, adding a splash more oil if needed, and cook the onions and garlic gently for 10 minutes, until softened. Add the green chillies (deseeding them, if liked) and the sugar and spices, stirring for 2 minutes.

Tip in the tomatoes, stock and juice of the orange and 1 lime, then bring to a gentle simmer. Return the meat to the pan, along with any juices. Cover with a tightly fitting lid and simmer gently for 2 hours, stirring occasionally.

By now the pork should be falling apart. Lift the steaks from the pan and shred with two forks. Chop the sweet potatoes into 1 cm chunks, then add to the pan along with the shredded meat. Simmer uncovered for another 35–40 minutes, stirring regularly so it doesn't stick to the bottom of the pan. Drain and rinse the kidney beans, then stir through and simmer again for about 10 minutes, until the potatoes are completely tender and everything is coated in a thick sauce.

Squeeze over the juice of the remaining lime, scatter with the coriander then serve with the Corn and Chilli Slaw and either brown rice or warm crusty wholemeal bread.

Note: Instead of serving with rice, try piling the chilli over baked sweet potatoes (leave them out of the meat mixture in this case).

SERVE WITH THE CORN AND
CHILLI SLAW (PAGE 227)

VENISON STEAKS WITH GRIDDLED CHICORY

SERVES 4 **PREPARE** 10 MINS PLUS MARINATING **COOK** 20 MINS

4 venison steaks
(about 125–150g each)

6 tbsp balsamic vinegar

300ml red wine

2 medium heads white chicory,
trimmed and halved lengthways

2 medium heads red chicory,
trimmed and halved lengthways

1 tbsp olive oil

1 clove garlic, crushed

Half a bunch of fresh thyme,
roughly chopped, plus extra
to garnish (20g)

361 Kcal
1509 kJ

Venison is the best of both worlds – lean but still really tasty.

This is the perfect dinner party dish when served with griddled chicory or celeriac mash (from Venison with Blueberry Sauce | page 206 |), and green beans on the side.

Place the venison steaks in a large bowl and pour over 2 tbsp each of the balsamic vinegar and red wine. Allow to marinate in the fridge for 1 hour.

Brush the chicory with the oil and cook on a hot griddle for 2 minutes on each side until softened. Remove from the pan and set aside.

Return the griddle to the heat and cook the venison for 6–8 minutes for medium, turning halfway through. Remove, set aside and cover to keep warm.

Add the garlic to the pan and cook for about 30 seconds, then add the thyme with the remaining vinegar and wine and cook until the glaze sauce is reduced by half.

Serve the chicory with the sliced venison arranged on top. Drizzle over the balsamic glaze. Serve with celeriac mash and green beans.

SALMON WITH APPLE, FENNEL & RADISH SALAD

SERVES 6 **PREPARE** 10 MINS PLUS COOLING **COOK** 20 MINS

For the salad:

50g blanched hazelnuts

1 Granny Smith or Pink Lady apple, cored and finely sliced

1 fennel bulb, trimmed, cored and finely sliced

100g radishes, trimmed and finely sliced

2 tbsp olive oil

1½ tbsp lemon juice

2 heads of chicory

1 tbsp roughly chopped dill

For the salmon:

6×100g salmon fillets

2 tbsp white wine vinegar

2 bay leaves

2 tsp fennel seeds

10 black peppercorns

250ml dry white wine

284 Kcal
1181 kJ

This fish dish is really fresh and fragrant, perfect for spring lunches, a party starter or a light evening meal after a heavy Sunday roast. The salmon is a source of omega-3 unsaturated fatty acids, a good addition to a healthy diet, which may also help protect our hearts.

Preheat the oven to 200°C/gas mark 6. Roast the hazelnuts on a baking tray for 5 minutes or until golden and smelling nutty. Leave to cool, then roughly chop.

Toss the apple, fennel and radishes together. Mix the oil and lemon juice, season and toss through the salad. Scatter with the chicory leaves, dill and the roasted nuts.

Meanwhile, place all the ingredients for the salmon, except the fish, in a shallow sauté pan or roasting tray with 400ml boiling water. Bring to the boil. Add the salmon in a single layer, cover and remove from the heat. Leave to stand for about 15 minutes, or until the salmon is just cooked. Remove the salmon from the liquid and serve whole or broken into large chunky flakes with the apple, fennel and radish salad.

Note: As an alternative to the poached salmon, serve with roast chicken breasts or a generous spoonful of fresh crab, allowing about 75g per person.

You can prepare the salmon 24 hours beforehand and keep it in the fridge.

SALMON IS A GOOD SOURCE OF
OMEGA-3 UNSATURATED FATTY ACIDS

233 ♡

HARISSA SPATCHCOCK CHICKEN & ROCKET SALAD

SERVES 4 **PREPARE** 15 MINS **COOK** 50 MINS

2 tbsp harissa paste

2 tbsp light olive oil

1 small whole chicken
(about 1.4–1.6kg)

2 lemons

100g rocket

80g spinach

100g watercress

30g queen olives, sliced

A bunch of fresh flat-leaf parsley,
leaves picked (25g)

396 Kcal
1655 kJ

*These Moroccan flavours make for a lovely summer lunch when
served with a variety of salads.*

Preheat the oven to 220°C/gas mark 7. In a small bowl, mix together
the harissa paste with 1 tbsp of the olive oil.

Spatchcock the chicken: turn the chicken over, breast side down and,
using kitchen or poultry scissors, cut along both sides of the backbone
to remove it. Turn the chicken over and press down to flatten.

Rub the harissa and oil generously over the chicken. Place the chicken
on a rack over a deep roasting tray. Add the zest and juice of 1 lemon.

Place the chicken in the hot oven to roast for 15 minutes. Turn the heat
down to 180°C/gas mark 4 and cook for a further 35 minutes, until the
skin is crisp and golden, the juices run clear when the thickest part of
the chicken is pierced with a skewer and there is no pink meat.

To make the salad, using a sharp knife or mandolin, thinly slice the
lemon and add to a bowl with the remaining ingredients and toss
to combine. Season and dress with a drizzle of the chicken juices
and serve.

Notes: Save time by buying a chicken already spatchcocked from
a good butcher.

You can start off cooking in the oven but finish on the barbecue for
the final 10–15 minutes. It's important to keep an eye on the chicken
to make sure it stays nice and juicy, but is cooked thoroughly.

BETTINA'S
STORY

"Bettina's story is an inspiration for us all. Her decision to adopt a healthy lifestyle through healthy cooking is one of the most important non-drug measures to reduce blood pressure and to prevent cardiovascular disease, like heart disease, stroke and kidney failure.

Eating a diet low in salt and fatty foods and rich in fresh vegetables, fruits and fish is what we should all be striving for to ensure good health and normal blood pressure. Bettina's new approach will likely result in better control of her blood pressure and she may require less medication."

– BHF PROFESSOR RHIAN TOUYZ
University of Glasgow

My first impression of Bettina was an overwhelming sense of passion and positivity. When we met up, the Jamaican-born mother and grandmother couldn't wait to share her love of cooking and baking with me.

Bettina's story began when she was taken ill on her commute home. The next day she went to the doctor and discovered she had high blood pressure, a normally symptomless condition putting her at greater risk of heart attack and stroke.

Having witnessed the debilitating effects of high blood pressure while growing up – her mother suffered the same condition – the diagnosis came as a shock and prompted her to take control of her life and her health.

Bettina started creating healthy alternatives to all her favourite Caribbean recipes. For example, instead of cooking her Jamaican rice and peas with coconut milk, she used natural yoghurt, and began substituting salt with herbs and spices to season her dishes.

She told me how she wanted to turn her experience into something positive, and did so by volunteering with a BHF community project in her home city of Nottingham, sharing the message of heart health with local people.

Today Bettina has her blood pressure under control and enjoys nothing more than rustling up tasty and healthy meals for her family and friends.

ROASTED NECTARINES, ROSE YOGHURT & NUTS

SERVES 8 **PREPARE** 5 MINS **COOK** 30-60 MINS

8 nectarines, halved and stoned

50g soft dark brown sugar
or date syrup

Juice of 1 lime

1-2 drops rose water, or to taste

300ml 0% fat Greek yoghurt

75g pistachio nuts or hazelnuts,
roasted and chopped

2-3 tsp dried rose petals, to garnish

146 Kcal
610 kJ

A pretty and light dinner party dessert, particularly when the fruit is sweet and ripe. If you like, you could add fresh figs alongside the nectarines.

Preheat the oven to 190°C/gas mark 5. Arrange the nectarines in an ovenproof dish lined with baking parchment, placed cut-side up in a single layer. Sprinkle over the sugar and lime juice.

Pour 75ml cold water around the fruit and bake for 30-40 minutes. (How long it takes depends on how ripe your fruit is – ripe fruit cooks faster, hard fruit can take up to 60 minutes). Meanwhile, stir the rose water into the yoghurt.

Serve the roasted nectarines on the rose yoghurt, scattered with the pistachios or hazelnuts and a sprinkling of rose petals.

RHUBARB & CUSTARD SEMI FREDDO

SERVES 6 **PREPARE** 10 MINS PLUS COOLING & FREEZING **COOK** 10 MINS

500g forced pink rhubarb,
cut into 2 cm pieces

125g clear honey or agave syrup

2–4 tsp rose water

500g low-fat vanilla custard

150g Greek yoghurt (4% fat)

100g low-fat yoghurt

2 tbsp vodka, optional

191 Kcal
804 kJ

I love these classic English flavours with an Italian twist. Low-fat custard and yoghurt are an equally delicious but heart-healthy alternative to standard semi freddo or ice cream.

Place the rhubarb, honey or syrup and rose water in a small pan. Bring to the boil and simmer gently for 8–10 minutes until the rhubarb is just tender. Turn off the heat and leave to cool.

In a separate bowl, beat together the custard, yoghurt and vodka (if using) until smooth, using an electric whisk for speed. Gently ripple half the cooled rhubarb mixture through and set aside the remainder for later.

Pour the mixture into a 900g loaf tin lined with cling film. Cover and freeze for about 3–4 hours until solid, then turn out. Beat the mixture using a fork once or twice during freezing to break down the ice crystals as they form.

To serve, use a large sharp knife that has been dipped in hot water, and cut into thick slices. If frozen for more than 24 hours, transfer to the fridge for 20 minutes to soften before serving. Serve with the reserved rhubarb compote.

BERRY & ELDERFLOWER TARTS

SERVES 2 **PREPARE** 10 MINS **COOK** 10 MINS

3 sheets filo pastry

1 tbsp sunflower oil,
or melted sunflower spread

1 tsp elderflower cordial

50g 0% fat Greek yoghurt

150g strawberries, hulled,
or mix of seasonal berries

1 tbsp redcurrant jelly (30g)

Fresh mint to garnish

 383 Kcal
1616 kJ

The light and fragrant flavour of elderflower always reminds me of British summertime, especially when combined with seasonal berries. Filo pastry has an impressive finish and crunchy crust, while being lower in fat and saturated fat than shortcrust, puff or flaky pastry.

Preheat the oven to 190°C/gas mark 5. Lightly grease 2×12 cm loose-bottomed flan tins. Cut each filo sheet in half and trim to make 6×16 cm squares.

Brush a square with a little of the oil. Oil a second sheet and place on the first with the points at an angle, like petals. Repeat with the third sheet and press well into the tin. Repeat with the remaining tin and filo pastry.

Bake for 10 minutes or until browned and crisp. If the points are browning too quickly, cover lightly with foil.

When cool, carefully remove the pastry cases from the tins and place each onto a serving plate. Stir the elderflower cordial into the yoghurt, then spoon into the pastry cases.

Slice the strawberries (or berries), leaving any small ones whole, and arrange on top.

Melt the redcurrant jelly in a small saucepan with a teaspoon of cold water. Brush over the strawberries until generously coated. Garnish with mint before serving.

Note: Ensure you fill the pastry just before serving, otherwise the fruit can make the base go soggy.

BERRY ROULADE

SERVES 8 **PREPARE** 6–8 MINS **COOK** 10–15 MINS PLUS COOLING

3 medium eggs

100g golden caster sugar
plus extra for dusting

100g spelt flour

¾ tsp baking powder

200g raspberries

4 tbsp reduced-sugar raspberry
jam or No-Cook Chia Berry
Conserve | page 32 |

300g skyr or low-fat yoghurt

185 Kcal
783 kJ

If you're celebrating, this is a treat that everyone can enjoy. Better still, it's quick to prepare – just ensure you let it cool before adding the filling.

Preheat the oven to 200°C/gas mark 6. Line a shallow 23×32 cm Swiss roll tin with baking parchment.

To make the sponge, place the eggs and sugar in a large bowl and whisk with an electric mixer for 6–8 minutes until very pale in colour and thick enough to leave a trail on the surface when the whisk beaters are lifted.

Tip the flour and the baking powder into a sieve and sift over the whisked mixture. Fold in using a large metal spoon, cutting through the mixture until all traces of flour are gone. Using the back of a fork or spoon, crush 125g of the raspberries, then gently fold them through the mixture, so that they are evenly swirled.

Pour the mixture into the tin, spreading evenly into the corners. Bake for 10–15 minutes, until the cake is firm to touch. Turn out onto a clean sheet of baking parchment sprinkled with a little extra caster sugar. Peel off and discard the old baking parchment and roll up the Swiss roll, beginning at the short end and using the baking parchment to help you so that the cake is completely enclosed in the paper. Allow to cool.

When cool, unroll the sponge and spread with the raspberry conserve, spreading evenly and right up to the edges. Repeat with the skyr or low-fat yoghurt, then carefully re-roll the cake, using the paper to help. Trim the edges if required, transfer to a plate and serve dusted with caster sugar and the remaining fresh raspberries.

Note: Self-raising flour also works instead of the spelt flour and baking powder.

Other seasonal berries will also work in place of the raspberries – try blackberries, blueberries or chopped strawberries.

BLUEBERRY & POMEGRANATE GRANITA

SERVES 6 **PREPARE** 5 MINS PLUS FREEZING

500g fresh or frozen blueberries

4 tbsp clear honey or agave nectar

300ml pomegranate juice

To serve: pomegranate seeds and skyr or low-fat yoghurt

Mint leaves to garnish

114 Kcal
476 kJ

"I love the blueberry & pomegranate granita. It's really refreshing and the combination of both fruits is lovely – as well as giving you a portion of your five a day. These fruits also go really well together to make a delicious smoothie."

DAME KELLY HOLMES

A truly refreshing palate cleanser, granita is perfect if you love ice cream but want to avoid the cream and saturated fat that come with it.

Place all the ingredients in a blender and blend until smooth.

Pour into a shallow freezer-proof container or roasting tin and place in the freezer. Leave to freeze completely, stirring after 1–2 hours. This will take at least 6 hours, depending on your freezer.

Once fully frozen, scrape the surface of the ice with a sturdy fork and spoon the granita into serving dishes scattered with pomegranate seeds and mint and a spoonful of skyr or yoghurt on the side.

RASPBERRY POTS WITH RASPBERRY SAUCE

SERVES 4-6 **PREPARE** 20 MINS PLUS CHILLING TIME **COOK** 5 MINS PLUS COOLING TIME

400g fresh raspberries

75g clear honey or agave syrup

4 medium egg whites

300g low-fat yoghurt

6 sheets gelatine

156 Kcal
660 kJ

With all the indulgence of a mousse or chilled soufflé, but using yoghurt instead of cream, this recipe is wonderfully intense when paired with the raspberry sauce.

Make the raspberry sauce: reserve 12 of the raspberries to use to garnish, and place the remaining berries in a pan with half of the honey and gently cook over a medium heat for 4-5 minutes, stirring until the fruit collapses. Place a fine sieve over a bowl and pass the fruit through to deseed. Cool for 10 minutes, then keep in the fridge until needed.

In a clean bowl, whisk the egg whites for 2-3 minutes or until stiff peaks form. Then place the yoghurt in a bowl, stir in 200ml of the raspberry coulis and the remaining honey and beat to combine.

Soak the gelatine in cold water for 5 minutes, and drain well. Add 3 tablespoons of boiling water to the gelatine in a large jug and leave until the gelatine has dissolved. Add to the yoghurt mixture, then beat in a third of the egg whites. Fold in the remaining egg whites.

Gently divide the mixture between 4-6 tall glasses or mugs. Chill for 4-5 hours. To serve, decorate with reserved raspberries, with the remaining raspberry sauce in a small jug or ramekin on the side.

THANK YOU

All proceeds from this book will go to the BHF and will fund vital future heart research, helping to provide a better quality of life for millions of people with heart conditions.

INDEX